THE DIARY OF A 49er

Edited by Chauncey L. Canfield

High Grass Publications
PO Box 1979
Redmond, Oregon 97756

ISBN 0-9672561-0-0

DEDICATION

In memory of Ron Noonan, a good longshoreman and kindhearted man who showed many how to enjoy and dream through the books he lugged into the hiring hall.

May your Harry Lundsberg be spotless, cocked and always ready for cargo.

ACKNOWLEDGMENTS

Thanks to Zachary Pounds, Stoney Potter and Radical Randy for instilling in me their beliefs on freedom to do as you choose and the desire to see beyond the last shovel full.

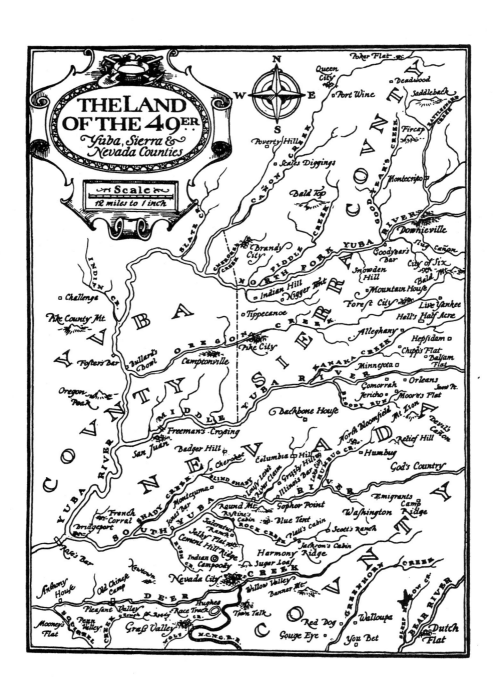

THE DIARY OF
A FORTY-NINER

Edited by

CHAUNCEY L. CANFIELD

To my wife, my chum for
a quarter of a century,
this book is lovingly
dedicated.

Chauncey L. Canfield.

❧ CONTENTS ❧

CHAPTER I.................................Page 1

The Hardships of a Miner's Life—Letters From Home
—The Express Rider and His Welcome Call—The
Beginnings of Nevada City—Tapping a Monte Bank—
A Fascinating Twenty-One Dealer—Wingdaming
the River—An Indian Funeral Ceremony—The Ups
and Downs of Mining—The Advent of the Long-Tom
on Rock Creek.

CHAPTER II.................................Page 15

Bunking With Pard—A Rich Claim—The First Ground
Sluice—Siestas Under the Big Pine—Naming the Town
—A Dog Fight and a Purchase—The Grass-Widow
Secures a Mate—A Shivaree and its Consequences—
Banished From Selby Flat—Anderson's Eccentricities.

CHAPTER III.................................Page 23

A Rattlesnake on the Trail—Claim Jumping and a
Tragedy—Miners' Courts and the Alcalde—Raising
the Anti-Debris Question—The First Sermon and a
Liberal Collection—A Welcome Storm—Pack Mule
Load of Coarse Gold—Riparian Rights—An Expensive
Chicken Broth—Begging Letter From North.

CHAPTER IV.................................Page 33

The Forest in Autumn—A Sluice Robber and the Whipping Post—North as a Monte Dealer—An Encounter
With a Highwayman—High Priced Hay—Another

Meeting With the Frenchwoman—Mexicans Discover a Big Bonanza—An Eviction by Force—Recognition of the Rights of Foreign Miners.

CHAPTER V.................................Page 43
Weather Contrasts—Anticipating the Exhaustion of the Placers—A Lively Dance at Selby Flat—The Fight Between the Jackass and the Ferocious Bear—Decamping Showmen—The Town Celebrates the Event —A Foothill Ditty—The Murder of Henry North— Following the Channels Under the Mountain—The Growth of Nevada City.

CHAPTER VI.................................Page 53
A Real Estate Speculation—Encounter With a Road Agent—Discovery of Rich Quartz Veins at Grass Valley—A Valuable Specimen—Madame Ferrand Visits Rock Creek—Rich Diggings on the North Yuba—Generosity of the Pioneers—The Twenty-One Dealer's Fortune.

CHAPTER VII.................................Page 61
A Trip to San Francisco—Speculating in Sandhill Lots —High Living—Hetty Breaks the Engagement—Back in the Claim—Nevada County Organized—Drawing Money From a Gravel Bank—More Gold Discoveries —The Rescue of a Party of Unfortunate Immigrants— The "Lost Grave."

CHAPTER VIII.................................Page 69
Murder on the Trail—A Pursuing Posse—Wanted, a French Dictionary—Caring for the Distressed Immigrants—Jackson's Confession—The Jolly Crowd at the Saleratus Ranch—A Midnight Concert and a Row— Haying in the Mountains—Letters From Home—The Old Folks Taking it Easy—A Peace Persuader—Pard's Disposition Changes for the Better.

CHAPTER IX..............................Page 79

Women Arriving in the Country—Our Hero Wrestles With the French Language—A Waiter Who Could Not Understand His Native Tongue—The Rival Fourth of July Celebration at Selby Flat—Close to a Lynching Bee—Pard Gets a Surprise—Forming a River Mining Company—The Sandhill Speculation Prospers —Anderson's Revelation.

CHAPTER X..............................Page 89

Fascination of the Sierra Foothills—An Ideal Friendship—Lousy Level—Jack and the Mountain Lion— The Burning Pine—Sawmill Invasion of the Forests— Mounting a Broncho—Cruel Punishment Dealt to Petty Thieves—Departure for the River.

CHAPTER XI..............................Page 99

Fluming the South Yuba—In the Bed of the Stream— A Picturesque Camp—Guarding the Gold Dust—Extending the Real Estate Speculation—Jackson Forms the Reading Habit—The Fascination of the "Three Musketeers"—A Reformation at Selby Flat—An Experimental Vegetable Garden on Rock Creek—The Biggest Poker Game to Date.

CHAPTER XII..............................Page 107

A Trip to the Mountains—An Experience in a Sierra Snowstorm—Perils of the North Fork Canon—An Opportune Find of a Deserted Cabin—Entertainment For Man and Beast—The Return to Rock Creek—Hospitable Miners—Discovery of the Big Blue Lead— Opening the Ancient River Channels.

CHAPTER XIII..............................Page 117

Setting Sluice Boxes—Promised Christmas Feast at Selby Flat—The First Newspaper Established—Hermit Platt Tells His Story—A Pioneer Overland Expedition Across the Arid Arizona Deserts—Perils and Dangers of the Journey—A Welcome Oasis—Arrival at Don Warner's Ranch—Sad News Awaits the Argonaut at San Francisco.

CHAPTER XIV...................................Page 125

A Sensation on the Flat—The Mysterious Disappearance of the Turkeys—The No-Gobbler Bettors Win Their Wagers—An Angry Landlord—The Saleratus Ranch Under Suspicion—Just a Plain, Every-Day Dinner—The Rendezvous and a Feast Down the Creek—The Sweetheart Delays Her Return—The Jackass Escapes a Serenade.

CHAPTER XV...................................Page 131

Strange Disappearance of Carter and Ristine—A Deserted Shanty—Ristine's Death—Revelations at the Inquest—Who Stole the Turkeys?—A Rich Streak on the Bed-Rock—Pard Bars the Banjo—Hetty has a Change of Heart—The Interior of a Miner's Cabin—A Sentimental Picture—Friendship, Prosperity, and Contentment.

CHAPTER XVI...................................Page 141

The Raging Yuba—A Visit to the River—Bad Case of Jim-Jams—A Swarm of Tin Jacketed Imps—Sunday in Nevada—Food Famine in the Mining Camps—Rattlesnake Dick Shoots Up the Town—A Quartz Mining Speculation and its Failure.

CHAPTER XVII...................................Page 149

A Formidable Indictment of the Turkey Thieves—An Old-Time Legal Document—Haled into Court—The Trial; the Verdict and the Penalty—A Safety Valve for the Wild Spirits—The Jackass Not For Sale—

Pard's Tender Heart—His Consideration for Bird and Beast and Affection for His Cabin Mate—The Donkey's Correct Principles.

CHAPTER XVIII...........................Page 157

Jackson Visits the Neighboring Mining Camps—Pocket Hunting at Rough and Ready—A Puzzle for the Theorists—A Section of a Dead River—Speculation on the Genesis of Gold—The Old-Timers' Dictum—First Visit to the Theater—Pard Returns From San Francisco—A Profitable Investment—Jackson Decides to Marry His French Sweetheart.

CHAPTER XIX.............................Page 165

Pard Brushes Up in His Profession—No Deference Paid to Wealth—How Fortune Favored Jenkins—When You Have Got the Luck, It's With You From Start To Finish—Jim Vineyard's Hard Streak—A Moving Tale of a Missed Opportunity—One Man's Loss Another Man's Gain—Trousers Pockets vs. Money Belts.

CHAPTER XX..............................Page 171

The Unsociable Couple on Round Mountain—Good Fellowship Among the Pioneers—The Tax-Collector Passes the Miners By—A Woman in Breeches—Marie Returns From France—Adoption of a New Method of Sluicing—The Dog and Donkey Strike up a Friendship —Frank Dunn and His Eccentricities—Posing as a Horrible Example.

CHAPTER XXI.............................Page 181

A Successful Experiment—A Joke on the Visitors— Road Agents Hold Up a Stage—Unchivalric Treatment of the Woman Passenger—Meeting of the Lovers— Jackson's Word Picture of the Beauties of the Landscape, Viewed From Sugar Loaf—The Reconciliation of Anderson and Wife—Marie's Comments.

CHAPTER XXII..........................Page 189

A Placid Life—Marie Observes the Proprieties—Pard
Plans for the Future—The Progress of a Love Idyll—
Reelfoot Williams and His Gang—Jack's Warning—
Robbery of the Blue Tent Store—A Fruitless Pursuit—
Negotiating the Sale of Mining Properties—Shallow
Placers Worked Out and Deep Diggings Take Their
Place.

CHAPTER XXIII..........................Page 197

A Combination to Work Rock Creek—Extracting Gold
From Blue Cement—The Critical Cats at Selby Flat—
French Cooking in the Old Cabin—The Influx of China-
men into the Mines—A Joint Visit to Round Mountain
—Marie Predicts an Explosion—No Cause for
Interference.

CHAPTER XXIV..........................Page 205

The Partners Sell Out the Creek Claim—Jackson's
Reputation in His Old Home—Providing for the Jack-
ass's Future—The Slocum Farm Has No Attraction—
Loafing the Days Away—Rushes to New Localities—
Trouble on Round Mountain—Scandalmongers'
Tongues Let Loose—Chinamen Show Fight and are
Run Off of Deer Creek.

CHAPTER XXV..........................Page 213

Sad Termination of the Round Mountain Mystery—A
Suicide's Cynical Farewell—The Intrusion of the
"Eternal Feminine"—Pard's Remarks—"Let There Be
No Clack of Idle Tongues"—An Impressive Ceremony
and a Solitary Grave—The Partners Grow Sentimental
Over the Old Log Cabin and Their Mutual Experiences
—Preparing for a Leave-Taking.

CHAPTER XXVI.........................Page 219

Distributing Personal Effects—Pard's Farewell Dinner —"Zey Are Ze Good Boys"—Champagne and Its Effects —The Last Sitting Under the Old Pine Tree—Voices of the Night Chorus a Melancholy Farewell—Wind-up of Jackson's Diary—The Fate of Hetty and a Last Word in Regard to the Actors Who Have Figured in the Old-Time Record.

EPILOGUE..............................Page 227

THE DIARY OF
A FORTY-NINER

PREFACE

Now and again there comes out of the dim past something which opens up an hitherto unknown or forgotten page in history. A copper implement from a lake midden, a chipped arrow head from a cave, a deciphered hieroglyphic from the face of a granite rock, a ruined temple in an overgrown jungle by means of which we rescue a chapter that tells of men's works and men's lives, former generations, who cumbered the earth for a brief time and passed away and of whose existence even tradition is silent. There are fascinating revealments that excite a momentary interest only, for, barring the scientist, we live in the present, and how our remote ancestors throve or what they did gives us but little concern. The long ago is vague, the cave dwellers and the temple builders existed in fable land, and, while we concede the importance of the discoveries, we leave the study to the specialists and magazine writers and do not burden our mind with ancient history. This indifference not only obtains with reference to the tribes and peoples who have disappeared off of the earth; it is equally true of comparatively recent events.

Probably no one thing has had a greater influence upon the progress and expansion of our own country than the discovery of gold in California in 1849, following the material wealth that it added to the world's store. Figures of billion gold production have been recorded and preserved, but beyond that there is no authentic or truthful record. That unique period is without its historian, and in only a vague way is it comprehended. The present generation is content to adopt Bret Harte's tales as veracious chronicles of life in the foothills and mining camps of the "Fifties," yet every old

pioneer knows that his types were exaggerated, the miners' dialect impossible and unknown; but he illumined his pages with genius, he caught the atmosphere, and neither protest nor denial are sufficient to remove the belief that he was writing real history. As for the latter day romancers, who attempt to reproduce pioneer times, they are usually mushy imitators of Harte who romance without knowledge or understanding. Those old, free, careless days were and are without parallel. The conditions that created them vanished with the exhaustion of the shallow "diggings," and when in creek, gulch and ravine the golden harvest had been gathered life became prosiac and dull, with the dullness propriety asserted itself, the conventions of a more exacting social order crept in and the amazing foothill days of the "Fifties" existed only as legend and tradition.

Perhaps it was best. Men were getting dangerously close to Paganism, yielding to the beckoning of "the wild," the insidious climatic influence of the pine-clothed hills, and it was well that the shackles of civilization should again fetter them. A great empire demanded development, fertile valleys invited cultivation, and the "cow counties" (as the plains were contemptuously termed by the miners), with the decay of mining, began to assert their importance and supremacy. In the "Sixties" new conditions sprang into existence and finis was written to the characteristics of the days of "'49."

To write understandingly of that period one must have lived in it; to catch the spirit one must have been a part of it. In these prosy days of railroads and trusts it is a fable, resting on no better authority than the romancers' creations or senile maunderings of the belated pioneer. And yet the half has not been told. Then fact was romance and romance fact. To be rich was not to be envied, to be poor brought no reproach. Brawn and muscle counted for more than brains;

health and strength was a more available capital than a college education.

There lately came into possession of the editor of the text that follows this preface a stout, leather-bound book of some three hundred pages, containing a jumble of accounts and records of happenings and incidents ranging from the cost of provisions and supplies to notes of the doings of mining chums and neighbors. Bearing every evidence of genuineness, it purported to be the experiences of one Alfred T. Jackson, a pioneer miner who cabined and worked on Rock Creek, Nevada County, California. In the lapse of the fifty odd years since it had been written, the ink had faded and turned yellow, many of the lines were barely legible, and a dozen of the first leaves of the book had been torn away. Fortunately, the remainder was intact and the subject matter proved to be of vital historical interest. Here at last was a truthful, unadorned, veracious chronicle of the placer mining days of the foothills, a narrative of events as they occurred; told in simple and, at times, ungrammatical sentences, yet vivid and truth compelling in the absence of conscious literary endeavor. One speculates as to the motive that impelled the author to persist in his diary. He was not a Pepys, his naive confessions do not always give the real state of his mind or the true reasons for his actions. He was inclined to self-deception, was not frank with himself while pretending that its pages were intended only for his own eye. It is reasonable to believe that he entertained a lurking idea that it might see the light and this, with the relaxation it afforded him from a contemplation of his hardships and sordid surroundings, made it a pleasant Sunday evening task. At any rate, it is a unique contribution to the history of the era subsequent to the discovery of gold on the flanks on the Sierra Nevadas. It sets forth graphically the successive steps in gold mining, from the pan and rocker to the ground sluice and flume, and the

quaint belief of the pioneers that the placer gold deposits would soon give out, that the sojourn was but a transient one and that nothing then remained but a return to the "States." Equally interesting is the gradual evolution of the diarist, from the Puritanical New Englander, bound and shackled with the prejudices of generations, narrow and limited in his views and opinions, morally uncontaminated and unsophisticated in his experiences, to the broader and more typical Californian whose mental growth was stimulated by the freedom of his environment and associations. He becomes tolerant, worldly wise, more charitable to his fellowmen, convinced that over and beyond the horizon of the Litchfield hills, from whence he came, there was a world worth knowing and a life better worth living. The stay in the foothills made the at first alluring prospect of a return to his old home, even as the richest man in the village, not only irksome to contemplate, but impossible to endure.

That he was deeply indebted to "Pard," who was at one and the same time his mentor and friend, the record gives ample proof. Who among the old Californians that does not recall the instances of those wonderful friendships, resulting from like associations? "They cabined together in the 'Fifties'"; that signified a relationship, intimate and more self-sacrificing than that of brothers, a love that rose superior and forgave the irascibility resulting from toil, exposure and fatigue; that overlooked the exasperating repetition of sour bread and a scorching in the bean pot, and condoned the irritating effects of hard fare and rude shelter. Our hero convincingly illustrates the growth and strength of the affection that bound each to the other with "hooks of steel" and the interdependence their close companionship created.

No less fascinating is the romance interwoven in the pages of the diary. Its culmination, leaving the man on the threshold of a new life, while tantalizing in the vagueness of

what the future might be, does not admit of a doubt that this sturdy, self-reliant American was equal to a successful grapple with life's problems in whatever path he might take.

As a final word, the inside of the front cover bore the name of Alfred T. Jackson, Norfolk, Litchfield County, Conn., October 10, 1849. The entries range over a period of two years and the people referred to were persons who actually existed, not only in Nevada County, California, at the time covered by the diary, but also in his New England birthplace. The editor can add that the many incidents and happenings so simply noted, tragic and otherwise, have been verified, both by local tradition and the testimony of old timers still living, and that the diary gives a veracious, faithful and comprehensive picture of the pioneer miners' life in the early "Fifties."

THE DIARY OF
A FORTY-NINER

CHAPTER I.

THE HARDSHIPS OF A MINER'S LIFE—LETTERS
FROM HOME—THE EXPRESS RIDER AND HIS
WELCOME CALL—THE BEGINNINGS OF NE-
VADA CITY—TAPPING A MONTE BANK—A FAS-
CINATING TWENTY-ONE DEALER — WING-
DAMING THE RIVER—AN INDIAN FUNERAL
CEREMONY—THE UPS AND DOWNS OF MIN-
ING—THE ADVENT OF THE LONG-TOM ON
ROCK CREEK.

I

THE DIARY OF A FORTY-NINER

CHAPTER I.

MAY 18, 1850.—The pork I bought in town last night is the stinkenest salt junk ever brought around the Horn. It is a hardship that we can't get better hog meat, as it's more than half of our living. We fry it for breakfast and supper, boil it with our beans and sop our bread in the grease. Lord knows we pay enough for it. When I first settled on the creek it was a dollar a pound and the storekeeper talks about it being cheap now at sixty cents. I believe that if it were not for the potatoes that are fairly plenty and the fact that the woods are full of game, we would all die of scurvy. There is plenty of beef, such as it is, brought up in droves from Southern California, but it's a tough article and we have to boil it to get it tender enough to eat. There is a hunter who lives over on Round Mountain and makes a living killing deer and peddling the meat among the miners. He charges fifty cents a pound for venison steaks and he told me he made more money than the average miner. I paid seventy-five cents apiece in town yesterday for two apples and did not begrudge the money. I was told that they were grown in Oregon, which seemed strange, as I did not know that country had been settled long enough to raise fruit.

Will sell no more dust to M——. He allowed only $17.00 an ounce and then blew out two dollars' worth of fine gold; said it was not clean. Jerry Dix, who is only two claims above me on the creek, gets $18.50 for his at the store, but it

always weighs short. They are all in a ring to rob us poor miners. Sent an eleven dollar specimen home to dad.

Sack of flour	$14.00
Ten lbs. pork	6.00
One lb. tea	2.50
Ten lbs. beans	3.00
Two cans yeast powders	1.00
Five lbs. sugar	2.50
Codfish	2.00
Twenty lbs. potatoes	6.00
Five lbs. dried apples	1.50
Pair boots	16.00
Can molasses	3.00
Duck overalls	2.50
Shirt	2.00
Shovel	2.50
Pick	2 50
	$67.00

I was charged four dollars for delivering the lot at the creek Sunday morning. Forgot to get some powder and shot. Paid four bits apiece for two New York Heralds.

There is another man who is making money. All of our letters come by mail to Sacramento and are then sent by express to Hamlet Davis, the storekeeper on Deer Creek, who acts as postmaster, although he has no legal appointment. He is the big gold dust buyer of the camp and can afford to do the work for nothing, as it brings most of the miners to his store. Johnny Latham, the express rider, contracts to carry letters and papers for two bits each and rides the trails and creeks for miles around delivering them, beside selling newspapers to such as want the latest news from the

"States." We are always pleased when his mule heaves in sight and would gladly give him the weight of the letters in gold if we had to. How heartsick we get for news from the old home way off here out of the world and there is no disappointment quite as bad as when he passes us by without handing over the expected letter. My folks are mighty good; they never miss a steamer.

Everybody on the creek gone to town and it's pretty lonesome. I had to answer letters from Norfolk and that made me more homesick. I wonder what mother would say if she saw my bunk. Have not put in fresh pine needles for three weeks. I know she would like my bread; the boys all say I am the best bread baker on the creek. Wrote her a good long letter and sent dad the "Miners' Ten Commandments."

Wouldn't I like to be with them just for a day!

MAY 25, 1850.—Rocked sixty buckets each day during the week and got 7 1-2 ounces. Only worked half a day Saturday. Did not go to town. Sent over by Jim Early for some tobacco—five plugs for two dollars. Went hunting this morning; killed seventeen quail and four pigeons. They make a good stew if the rotten pork didn't spoil it, but it's better than the bull beef the butcher packs around. Took a snooze in the afternoon till the squawking of the blue jays woke me up. I don't mind them so much, but when the doves begin to mourn it seems as if I couldn't stand it. I get to thinking of dear old mother and dad and the old place, and wondered what they were all doing. I know. They went to church this morning and then set around and did nothing until chore time. I'll bet they didn't forget me.

I hear there are three women over on Selby Flat. Selby's brother, keeping a boarding house, and a grass-widow from Missouri, a skittish old woman who is looking for another

husband. The camp has more people than the settlement at Caldwell's store on Deer Creek.

What we miss more than anything else is that there are no women in the country, or comparatively few. Barring out the greasers and the squaws, I don't suppose there are twenty in all of Yuba County, outside of Marysville. With few exceptions they are of no particular credit to their sex. To one who was born and brought up where there were more women than men, it is hard to realize what a hardship it is to be deprived of their company. To hear some of the miners talk— the married ones—you would think their wives were angels, and maybe they were, but I guess it is because they are so far away. Still, when I recall Hetty North, it seems as if she was the dearest girl in the world, and, although we used to have lots of quarrels and tiffs and broke off our engagement a dozen times, I don't believe we would have a cross word if she were here with me now.

JUNE 1, 1850.—Claim paying pretty well. Washed out over five ounces, beside two nuggets, one nine and one eleven dollars. Could do better if the water did not bother so much. Got two long letters from home. Thank God, they are all well, or were a month ago. Dad got the two hundred I sent him; says I musn't stint myself to send money home. The neighbors think I am making a big fortune and many of the boys are planning to go to California this summer. Henry North has sold a yoke of oxen and his three-year-old colt, and starts next month. That is this month and he must be on the way. I like Henry, but I care more for his sister Hetty. I wonder if she will wait as she promised, until I get back. Baked enough bread to last until Saturday. Anderson spent the evening at the cabin. He is crazy on river mining. He and friends have located claims on the Yuba and are going to turn the

(NOTE: The camp at Caldwell's store grew into the present Nevada City.)

river when the water runs low. He is certain if he can get down on bed-rock he will take out gold by the bucketful. Wants me to join the company.

JUNE 8, 1850.—Went to town yesterday afternoon. With last week's washings I had eighteen ounces besides the nuggets. Spent $27 at the store and deposited $200. Had two bully meals at the hotel; first pie I have eaten since I got here. The town is full of drunken miners. Have kept my promise to mother and have not touched a drop since I started. Went into the Bella Union gambling saloon. The place was full and running over with gamblers and miners, and the latter seemed to be trying to get rid of their money as fast as possible. At some of the tables they were playing for high stakes, as much as one hundred dollars on the turn of a card. Monte was the most popular game and while I was there "Texas Bill" tapped one of the banks for two thousand dollars and won on the first pull. Then he took the dealer's seat and the banker quit until he could raise another stake.

There was a young French woman dealing twenty-one. She was as pretty as a picture. Began betting just to get near her and hear her talk. I lost seventy dollars and she did not notice me any more than she did the rest of the crowd. What would Hetty say if she knew I gambled? Four days' hard work gone for nothing!

JUNE 15, 1850.—Worked but three days last week. Had the cholera morbus pretty bad, but some Jamaica Ginger fetched me around all right. Took out just two ounces. Henry North wrote me a letter from San Francisco. He was broke and wanted enough money to come here. Sent him fifty dollars. I'll be glad to see him. Got a long letter

(NOTE.—"Tapping the bank" was the wagering by an outsider of an amount equalling the cash backing the game. Bets were usually limited to fifty dollars a single bet, but flush gamblers would often dare the dealer to accept a wager decided by a single deal of the cards, which if won doubled the bank's capital or broke it.)

from dad. He says mother is grieving about me being so far away and is afraid I will fall into temptation. She knows from what she sees in the papers that California must be an awful wicked place. Dad tells her that I come from old Connecticut stock and he isn't afraid of his boy not coming out all right. Wonder what he'd say if he knew about my losing money in a game of chance.

I hear that Anson James and his partner took out fourteen hundred dollars on Brush Creek last week. That beats Rock Creek, but Brush is all taken up. Anderson is after me to go river mining with him. He is getting up a company of ten men; has seven now and they will put up two hundred and fifty dollars apiece for capital. They want that for lumber, which costs one hundred dollars a thousand, and they need twenty thousand feet for wingdam and a flume, whatever that means. If my claim gives out before August, may go with them. Saw two deer on the hill back of the cabin and Anderson says a grizzly was killed up at the head of the creek last week. There are thousands of wild pigeons in the woods, but they are not fit to eat. The acorns they feed on makes their flesh taste bitter.

JUNE 22, 1850.—Have not heard from Henry North. He ought to have been here last week. I have been fairly homesick all the week, working in the claim alone, and I am so dead tired when night comes that it's a task to cook supper, although there isn't much to cook. There is always a pot of cold beans and I fry a piece of pork for the grease, to sop my bread in, and make a cup of tea. I roll up in the blankets and go to bed at eight o'clock and try to get to sleep just to keep from thinking, although I can't always do it. Thoughts of the old home will come into my head and it brings up everything that has happened since I was a boy. The frogs croak down in the creek just as they did on Norfolk Pond,

and it's the lonesomest sound on earth, barring the doves. There is a sort of a dog here that the greasers call a coyote, and you would swear when night comes on that there were a thousand of them yelping in the hills and around the cabin. Sometimes I get up and go outdoor, out under the stars, and wonder what Hetty is doing and whether she will wait. If she saw me sniffling and the tears rolling down my cheeks she would think I wasn't much of a man. I wish Henry North would come—it wouldn't be so lonesome. Rich diggings have been found on Kanaka Creek and a lot of miners have gone over to take up claims. Took out a little over five ounces for the week.

There is an Indian campoody up on the ridge above Brush Creek, where about two hundred Digger Indians are camped. They are the dirtiest lot of human beings on earth. One has to be careful going near the place, or he will surely get the itch. They will eat anything, acorns, grasshoppers, or seeds, and I have seen an old squaw pull a rotten pine log apart hunting for a white grub as big as my little finger, and, when she found one, swallow it alive with as much relish as if it were a fat oyster. There are two white men who have taken squaws to live with them in their cabins down on the river, but it is looked on as a disgrace and no decent miner will associate with them. The Indians burn their dead and I went over to the ridge with Jim Gleason to a buck's funeral Friday night. It was a queer ceremony. They piled up a cord or more of pine limbs, wrapped the buck in a blanket, deposited his body on the pile, together with his bow and arrows, clothes and small belongings, and set it on fire. The bucks of the tribe set around outside in the shadows, glum and silent as ghosts. The squaws joined hands and kept up a stamping, first with one foot and then the other, wailing together in a mournful chorus, which sounded like "wallah tu nae" and which they repeated over and over as long as I

9

stayed there. Others replenished the fire with fresh pine knots and limbs. The main attraction was an old, ugly squaw, who, I was told, although no relation to the buck, was chosen chief mourner. She went into a frenzy, howling and screeching like mad, contorting and twisting her body and spinning round and round until she exhausted herself and tumbled to the ground. Then she would come to and crawl to the fire, get hold of a piece of wood out of which the pitch was frying and daub it over her head and face until her hair was saturated with tar. They say that she never washes herself or tries to get the pitch off, and the buck's wife can't take another man until the tar wears away. It got to be monotonous and disgusting and I came away by midnight, but the Indians kept it up two nights, or until the last vestige of the body was burned up. What heathens they are to dispose of their dead in such a barbarous way instead of burying them decently in the ground!

JUNE 29, 1850.—This last week was my lucky one. Wednesday I struck a crevice in the bed-rock on the rim of the creek and it was lousy with gold. It took me two days to work it out and I got almost twenty-nine ounces, which with three ounces rocked the first two days raised the week's work to more than five hundred dollars. Sent dad seven hundred dollars last night. That makes twelve hundred dollars that he has of my savings. The strike helped me to get rid of the homesick feeling that has made me miserable for two weeks. Seems to me old Litchfield is nearer than it was, and I may fetch it before the rains come. The only thing bothering me is that the claim is almost worked out and I'll have to hunt new diggings soon. Strange I haven't heard from North since I sent him that fifty dollars. I got a letter from Hetty, however, the first I have received, asking me to look after him. Said he was weak and easily led. This is no

place for weaklings, but I'll take care of him for her sake. Had two square meals in town yesterday. They put me out of face with my regular grub.

JULY 6, 1850.—Been in town all day. The citizens had a celebration Friday, but it did not amount to much. Lawyer McConnell made a speech and another fellow read the Declaration of Independence. Then everybody fell into line, marched up and down the street, hurrahing and firing off pistols, and that was all there was to it. The town was jammed with outsiders and the hotels and restaurants ran short of grub. The saloons and gambling houses were chock-a-block and half the men in sight were full of rot-gut whiskey. Went in to see the pretty French woman, but could not get near the table where she was dealing. She's a handsome woman and the boys say she's straight as a string. That may be, but it is strange, considering the company she keeps and her occupation. Went home early, as I couldn't get a meal. It was so hot it was just simmering and I took a snooze under the big pine in front of the cabin. There was a fellow picking a banjo and singing a song in town to-day and it kept running in my head. It was about "Joe Bowers from Pike." The second verse was:

> I used to love a gal there, they called her
> Sally Black,
> I axed her for to marry me, she said
> It was a whack;
> But, ses she to me, Joe Bowers, before
> We hitch for life,
> You ought to have a little home to
> Keep your little wife.

If I can save enough money to buy the Slocum farm next to our place and Hetty says "yes," I'll have that "little home

and little wife" and that will be about all I want on this earth. I would like to have enough capital so that I would not have to slave from sunrise till dark as I did on dad's farm. I don't know as the work was any harder than what we do here, but there is a difference. There all we got was just about a bare living, at the best a few hundred dollars put away for a year's work, but here one don't know what the next stroke of the pick, or the next rocker full of dirt, may bring forth—an ounce or twenty ounces it may be. That is the excitement and fascination that makes one endure the hardships, working up to one's knees in cold water, breaking one's back in gouging and crevicing, the chance that the next panful will indicate the finding of a big deposit. That's the charm and it would be a great life were it not for the nights and the lonely cabin with only one's thoughts for company. It brings up to my mind a piece I used to recite at school. "Oh, solitude! where are the charms that sages have seen in thy face?" It's deadly lonesome and there are times when it seems as if I just could not stand it any longer. Baked two big loaves of bread in the Dutch oven. That will last through the week.

JULY 20, 1850.—Two weeks since I took up my pen. My hands are all calloused and I can do better work with a shovel than writing diaries. Have had bad luck; only cleaned up a little over four ounces and the claim is pretty near played out. Anderson offers me a share in his claim. He's working on a dry gulch just about half a mile north of the cabin. It's rich on the bed-rock, but he has to strip off about ten feet of top dirt and then pack the gravel down to the creek a couple of hundred yards. He offers me one-half a share in the ground if I will help him cut a ditch from the creek to the claim to carry the water to it. We will have to dig about a quarter of a mile. He says there is a new way of taking out

gold by a machine called a Long Tom. He saw it working at Kellogg's claim on Brush Creek and as much dirt can be put through it in a day as one can with a rocker in a week. I will go over and look at it to-morrow. Anderson is a good fellow and the only one on the creek I care much about. He is from Syracuse, New York, and has a good education. If I take his offer we will cabin together and it won't be so lonesome. Haven't heard a word from North and I don't know where to write him.

CHAPTER II.

BUNKING WITH PARD—A RICH CLAIM—THE FIRST
GROUND SLUICE—SIESTAS UNDER THE BIG
PINE—NAMING THE TOWN—A DOG FIGHT
AND A PURCHASE—THE GRASS-WIDOW SE-
CURES A MATE—A SHIVAREE AND ITS CONSE-
QUENCES—BANISHED FROM SELBY FLAT—
ANDERSON'S ECCENTRICITIES.

A FORTY-NINER

CHAPTER II.

JULY 27, 1850.—I went over and saw the Long Tom working. It will revolutionize mining if it will save the gold. Took plans of it. I'm handy with tools and knocked one together without much trouble. The Nevada blacksmith charged me four dollars to punch the holes in the sheet-iron plate. Set it up on the claim Friday and took out about two ounces that day. Worked a strip eight feet square. That is as much as I did in a week with a rocker. All the miners up and down the creek came to see it working. I had offers of two ounces apiece to make three of them, but I've promised Anderson to begin work on the ditch as soon as I get through with the claim. Had a letter from dad that gave me the blues. Dear old mother is ailing and pining to see me—afraid something will happen to me. Well, I am way off out of the world, but I've got the best of health. I wrote her a long letter cheering her up and promising I would come back as soon as I got six thousand dollars together. Dad says Hetty is a good girl and I could not pick out a better wife and that she comes over to the place regularly and asks them to read to her my letters. Some of the married miners are planning to bring their wives out from the States. About the only thing holding them back is the certainty that it will not take long to clean up all the gold there is in the country and then there would be nothing left to do except to go back again. A lot argue that they can go to farming in the valleys; but with the mines

worked out and the miners gone out of the mountains, where would they have a market for what they raised?

AUGUST 3, 1850.—Had a great streak of luck last week. Worked out the claim and before I moved the Tom, tried some of the rocker tailings. They were as rich as if the dirt had not been washed and I took nineteen ounces out of the riffle box beside a nugget that weighed nearly an ounce. I've taken out of the claim about one hundred and twenty ounces and have sent dad fifteen hundred dollars. It's cost me about five hundred dollars to live and I've got six ounces in the yeast powder box under the big stone in front of the fire place. Am worried about North. I don't care for the fifty dollars, but it's singular that he doesn't show up or write.

AUGUST 10, 1850.—Anderson moved his traps over to my cabin and we are living together. It makes a lot of difference having a pard with you, somebody to talk and tell your troubles to, although he laughs at me, swears that I have no troubles and don't know what troubles are. I have told him about the old folks and Hetty and about my plan to buy the Slocum farm, and he says: "Don't worry about the girl, she will wait for you fast enough as long as you are sending home money; and as for troubles, when you are married then you will begin to know something about them." I asked him if he was married and he said "yes" and then shut up like a clam. We have dug more than half the ditch and will finish it this week. There are a couple of gray squirrels that frolic around in the big pine tree near the cabin. I got the shotgun out, but Anderson said: "Why kill God's creatures? Let them live their lives." He's strange in some things. He laid there half the afternoon, watching them scampering around the limbs or setting up on their hind legs eating pine nuts, and said there was more satisfaction in enjoying their antics than eating squirrel stew.

A FORTY-NINER

AUGUST 17, 1850.—We finished the ditch on Thursday and turned in the water. It carries a lot more than we need and when we ran it into the gulch, Anderson got a new idea. We put a trench down through the middle of the ravine and there was a pretty heavy fall. The top dirt is nothing but red clay and he began picking the dirt and watching it run off into the creek and then he said: "What is the use of shoveling this all off when the water will do it for us?" Sure enough, it worked like a charm. We pulled off our shoes, turned up our overalls, jumped into the trench and worked away like beavers, and the water did more work in one day than both of us could have stripped shoveling in a week.

By Saturday noon we had cleared off a strip forty feet long and ten feet wide, and will set the Long Tom to-morrow and clean it up. It looks like pretty good ground, as we could pick up lots of pieces of gold, some of them weighing two bits.

The weather is awfully hot; believe it is warmer than summer in the States, but it don't bother us much to work when it's the hottest and I have not heard of anybody being sunstruck. It's curious how quickly it cools off after sundown. A breeze starts and blows up the creek strong enough to sway the tops of the pine trees, and the noise it makes through the branches sounds like a lullaby. Since Pard came to camp with me, we spend an hour or two every evening after supper sitting out under a big sugar pine that grows just in front of our cabin, smoking our pipes, but we don't talk much. It is all so solemn and still, that is, it seems so until you begin to hear what Pard calls "voices of the night"; the frogs, the owls, the rasp of the tree toad, or the howl of a wolf way off in the mountain, and if it was not for the glimmer of a light in Platt's cabin, down the creek, we would think

(NOTE.—Anderson had stumbled on another great step in mining, viz., ground sluicing, and without doubt was one of the first to adopt this method.)

19

we were two castaways lost in a wilderness. I believe it is that sort of feeling that drives so many of the boys to drinking, or carousing around the saloons hunting excitement.

AUGUST 24, 1850.—This last week was fine. We set the Tom Monday morning, put a box at the head of it and were three days and a half washing out the ground, which was about two feet thick; cleaned up the bed-rock and we got sixty-three ounces. We stripped off about thirty feet more by noon yesterday and will begin washing to-morrow. Anderson insisted on my taking half. I thought I ought to pay him something for the share in the claim. He wouldn't listen; said we were partners and he was bound to see that I got that Slocum farm and Hetty, just to teach me that there was trouble in the world. He gets letters from home, but they don't seem to give him much comfort. He reads them, swears under his breath, tears them in bits and sulks for the rest of the day. I sent a draft for five hundred dollars to the old folks last night. That is two thousand dollars I've saved in less than six months.

A woman who kept a boarding house at Selby Flat was killed yesterday. She got tangled in a lariat and was dragged to death by a mule.

We walked down to the Yuba River yesterday. There are about 200 miners working on the bars and banks, and they are doing pretty well. None of them have been able to get into the bed of the stream, as there is no way of turning the water. Anderson says there is no use of trying it now, as the rains would come before we could get to work, but he believes there is gold by the bucketful if he could get at it. We bought about a hundred dollars' worth of grub Saturday. There is a little beast here they call a woodrat and he plays the devil with anything left exposed about the cabin.

A FORTY-NINER

AUGUST 31, 1850.—Washed up two days and sluiced top dirt the rest of the week. The ground is still rich. We got forty-one ounces. That is as well as they are doing over on Brush Creek.

I bought a new suit of clothes yesterday, black broadcloth; two white shirts; a Peruvian hat and a pair of fine boots. The hat cost sixteen dollars, the boots twenty-one dollars, and the whole outfit, with necktie and handkerchiefs, one hundred and five dollars. I put them on this morning and went to town. Pard said I looked like a sport. It's so long since I wore decent clothes that I felt like a fool. I was told that the people living round Caldwell's store held a meeting and called the place "Nevada City." Nevada is Spanish for snow. The Frenchwoman is still dealing twenty-one. I went in to see her and started to make a bet when she said: "You can't play at this game. Gamblers are barred." I stammered out that I wasn't a gambler, but she said: "You can't play that on me," and I quit. She's got a voice like music and just her speaking to me in that way put me all in a flutter. There are a few women in the town, mostly Mexicans.

There was a dog fight down on the bridge and a lot of money bet on it. The losing dog was pretty badly chewed up, his forelegs bitten through and through, but he never whimpered. His owner was disgusted and swore he would kill him. I asked him what he would take for the dog, and I got him for two ounces. He could not walk and I had to carry him. My new boots hurt me like sin and by the time I got to the top of Sugar Loaf hill I had to take them off and walk over two miles in my stocking feet carrying my boots and the dog. When I got to the cabin my new clothes were a sight, but Anderson never laughed. He set to work washing the blood off the dog and binding up his legs. When I told him the story he said I was a good fellow and that the look out of the

dog's eyes and the way he licked my hand was worth more than I paid for him.

SEPTEMBER 7, 1850.—We took out only thirty ounces this past week. The gulch is getting narrow and there is a scant fifty feet more before we reach the ditch. There is a flat of about half an acre where the gulch runs out into the creek, and Anderson says the channel must run through it. If it does, we will have at least another month's work. There was some fun over on Selby Flat last week. A young fellow got stuck on the grass-widow and they went to town and got married. She is at least thirty years older than her husband, and when the boys got wind of it they gathered and gave the couple a shivaree. He got mad and turned loose a shotgun at the crowd, peppering some of them with bird shot. Then they corraled him and come pretty near lynching him. The boys say they would for sure, but the old woman got down on her knees and begged them to spare her dear husband. She prayed so hard that they agreed to let him go providing both would leave the camp the next morning. They skipped at night and now there is only one woman left on the flat and about three hundred men. Anderson says one woman is enough to keep the camp a-boiling. I can't make Anderson out. He's as good a chap as ever lived, kind-hearted, has no bad habits, always ready to do twice his share of the work if I would let him; but he doesn't seem to have any faith in anything or anybody except me. He gets letters from home regularly, reads them, swears and tears them up, and never talks about his life or his people. The dog is nearly well and Anderson is making a regular baby out of him. He says dogs are not like folks; they never go back on a friend. There is something on his mind that he broods over, but I do not see that I have any call to put my nose in his affairs, so I take no notice of his queer moods.

CHAPTER III.

A RATTLESNAKE ON THE TRAIL—CLAIM JUMPING AND A TRAGEDY—MINERS' COURTS AND THE ALCALDE—RAISING THE ANTI-DEBRIS QUESTION—THE FIRST SERMON AND A LIBERAL COLLECTION—A WELCOME STORM—PACK MULE LOAD OF COARSE GOLD—RIPARIAN RIGHTS—AN EXPENSIVE CHICKEN BROTH—BEGGING LETTER FROM NORTH.

23

A FORTY-NINER

CHAPTER III.

SEPTEMBER 14, 1850.—Claim is nearly played out. We cleaned up fifteen ounces last week and will work it out by Thursday. Sent five hundred dollars more to dad yesterday and I have got about three hundred on hand. I get the nicest kind of letters from dad. Mother is better because she thinks I will soon make enough to satisfy me and come back. Hetty says I ought to be there by Thanksgiving, but that is foolishness. If I am there by the next one I will be satisfied. I'm not so homesick since Anderson came to live with me. He is better educated than I am, has been through college and has had more experience, but he doesn't put on any airs and we get along together like brothers, although he has his blue spells. He never answers any letters that he gets, so far as I know, and those he receives are forwarded to him from San Francisco instead of coming here direct. He never goes to town, nor spends a cent except for grub. We killed a big rattlesnake on the trail to the claim Wednesday. It was coiled up under a bush and struck at and hit me on the bootleg. I jumped about ten feet and Anderson mashed its head with a stone. He was white as a sheet and called me a darned fool for not looking where I was going. I got mad and told him he need not worry about my not being able to take care of myself, then he put his arm around my neck and said he did not mean it; but I had come into his life and he did not want me to go out of it just yet. He's a character.

SEPTEMBER 20, 1850.—We finished up the claim last week. It about petered out. We got only five ounces. We are going to try the flat and if that don't pay we will go off prospecting. There was a fight on the creek last week. Donovan, an Irishman, jumped a claim, and when the rightful owner warned him off he drew an Allen's pepper box and shot Tracy, to whom the claim belonged, in the leg. Tracy beat the Irishman over the head with a shovel and left him for dead, although he did not die until yesterday. Tracy was taken over to town and tried before a fellow who sets himself up for an alcalde and was then turned loose, as it was a clear case of self-defense. This is the first death on Rock Creek. The miners are indignant over Tracy being taken to Nevada. There is no more law there than on Rock Creek. Some fellow claims to be a sort of judge, but he's got no legal authority and a miners' court is just as binding here as in town. We held a meeting of all the miners along the creek, and Anderson made a speech. Said it was an unwarranted usurpation and an invasion of our rights, and we resolved that we would not permit it to happen again. We buried Donovan on the hill, and sold his tools and traps at auction, including his cabin, for $140. Nobody knows what to do with the money, as it is not known where he came from. Anderson was made custodian of the proceeds in case any claimant should turn up.

SEPTEMBER 28, 1850.—We have worked on the ditch all the week, making it twice as large. The dirt on the flat

(NOTE.—An Allen's pepper box was a pistol much in vogue in the early days, a singularly ineffective gun, more dangerous to the possessor than anyone else. It got its name from its fancied resemblance to the old-fashioned pepper box. It had six barrels which revolved, and was a most clumsy piece of mechanism, although thousands were sold in the East to the early gold seekers. A joke of the times was a standing reward for proof that anyone had been hurt or wounded by its discharge. In a trial of a miner for assault with a deadly weapon and intent to kill, held before a sapient justice of the peace in Mariposa in 1851, the prisoner was discharged, the justice ruling that an Allen's pepper box could not be construed into as falling under the head of deadly or dangerous.)

it twenty feet deep and the more water we have the quicker we can sluice it off. I haven't much faith in its paying, although the bank on the creek prospects pretty well. I think Jack—that's our dog—is mighty ungrateful. I bought him and lugged him to the cabin when he couldn't walk and now he has got no particular use for me, but he just worships Anderson. Sleeps on the foot of his bunk nights, follows at his heels every minute of the day, or makes a bed of his coat alongside the claim; and if Anderson happens to get out of sight, howls and runs around like a crazy beast. When I mentioned it to Anderson he looked serious and said: "Don't get jealous, old fellow; you've got the folks at home and Hetty— I've got nothing but Jack, and a dog's love is better than none," and he walked out with the dog at his heels wagging his stump of a tail. I was completely upset. Anderson sat out under the pine tree for an hour with the dog's head in his lap and then came in cheerful-like, slapped me on the back and said: "Don't mind me being grumpy, I've got you too; but white man is mighty uncertain."

OCTOBER 5, 1850.—We turned the water into the ditch Monday and sluiced out the flat until Thursday. That afternoon a deputation of miners from below us on the creek came to the claim and notified us that we must quit. The mud we were sending down the stream buried them under slumgullion, and the water was so thick they could not use it in their rockers. Anderson said that was reasonable and that we would hold up until we could think of some scheme to remedy it.

We have talked it over and I don't see how we can avoid it unless we wait until the creek below is all worked out. The nights are cold and we have to keep up a fire in the fireplace. Kellogg was over from Brush Creek to look at our ditch.

(NOTE.—This is the first record of the raising of the anti-debris question.)

27

Says he is going to make a survey this week to bring the water into Brush Creek and if it is feasible he will give us four hundred dollars for the piece we have dug. They say he has made a pile of money and has bought up a lot of claims on Selby Hill.

OCTOBER 12, 1850.—There has not been a drop of rain, nor has there been a cloud in the sky since May last; but it thickened up early in the week and Tuesday night when I awoke the rain was pattering on the roof—a regular old-fashioned storm. Anderson woke up, too, and we got up and started a big fire and sat and listened to the gusts of wind blowing through the pine tree tops and sheets of water slapping up against the south side of the cabin. The rain sounded good. The whole country was dusty and dried up, and I felt as if I wanted to go out and stand bareheaded in the storm. It rained all day Wednesday, and Anderson, who went up to the claim in the afternoon, came back laughing and said he did not think the miners would bother us for a while on the slumgullion question. There was four feet of water in Rock Creek and rocks rolling down it as big as a bushel basket. It did not quit until Thursday afternoon. It washed out the head of the ditch and we have not fixed it up yet. Jack is in disgrace. He ran down a skunk Friday and we just couldn't stand him in the cabin until Anderson used up all of our soap washing him. He smells yet. We haven't made a dollar for two weeks.

OCTOBER 19, 1850.—We got the ditch repaired and the water turned on the flat by Thursday and have been running off the top dirt. It's amazing the amount we move and it astonishes all our neighbors. A lot of them are looking out for side hill diggings below us and will try the same process. Anderson says it will be a good idea to extend our ditch and

sell the water to the miners who might want to use it, but **I** don't see what right we have got to it more than anybody else. Anyway, he has put a notice at the head of the ditch claiming all the water it will hold, and as there is no law in the case he says he will make a law out of the precedent.

Had a letter from Henry North from Sacramento. Says he has been working there and has a great chance to make money if he had the capital. Asks me to loan him a thousand dollars. Anderson says to "go slow." I'd do it for Hetty's sake, but he ought to have written before this. A lot of miners have gone about forty miles north of here on another branch of the river where they say rich, coarse gold diggings have been discovered. A pack mule load of gold was brought into town from there last week and there was one piece worth three thousand dollars, and lots from an ounce to twenty ounces. Many of the miners think this is the discovery of the source of gold; that is, where it grows. There is one fact that bears out this theory. The higher the miners get up in the mountains, the coarser the gold. Around Nevada County, so far as I know, it is seldom that a nugget is found that weighs over an ounce, while up on Kanaka Creek one has been found that weighed twenty-one pounds and several from five to fifteen pounds, and I am told that there is very little fine dust in those diggings. I hope they won't find the fountain head until I have turned my gold into some kind of property.

OCTOBER 25, 1850.— We have had a great week. There is a streak up through the middle of our flat that is lousy with gold. We took out one hundred and eleven ounces and only worked a small portion of what we uncovered. We had a meeting of the miners at our place yesterday afternoon to decide in regard to ditch and water rights, and it was a hot one. Some of them claimed that water was as free as air and

(NOTE.—The first claim to water rights on record in Nevada County.)

no one had a right to monopolize it, and they would have carried the day, but Anderson proposed as a compromise that all interested should pitch in and build a ditch on shares. As there were only a dozen or so who had any use for the water outside of the creek bed, this was agreed to. These are the ones who have taken up flat claims like ours and are anxious to prospect them. We give our ditch to the company and have a one-sixth interest in the extension. I don't see what good it will do, but Anderson says common consent makes law and the action will establish our rights. Have had two good letters from home. Mother wants me to return for Thanksgiving and I'd like to be there, but the chances to get rich are too good to leave now. Dad writes that he has bargained for the Slocum Farm for four thousand dollars, and if I have another lucky week I will send him the balance. Somehow, I don't feel so eager to go back and live on it as I did three months ago.

NOVEMBER 3, 1850.—Another fair week, although not so good as the previous one. We are working the flat about forty feet wide and the sides do not pay as well as the middle streak, but we took out sixty-five ounces. The miners have been driven out of the creek bed by too much water and a great many have left for other diggings. There are two men cutting the extension to our ditch. Spent the day in Nevada City, as they call it now. There are over two thousand miners working in the vicinity of the town and most everybody doing well. My little Frenchwoman has gone away. I asked for her and they told me she was dealing over at Centerville.

There is no particular reason why I should be so much interested, although I was disappointed in not seeing her.

(NOTE.—The Grass Valley of to-day was first named Centerville because it was midway between the two more important mining towns of Rough and Ready and Nevada City.)

A FORTY-NINER

A minister preached in the United States Hotel dining room and the place was filled, but there were only three women in the crowd. I was told he took up a collection and raked in four hundred dollars. That is as good as mining and not as hard work. Our minister in Norfolk would be satisfied with that much for a year.

NOVEMBER 10, 1850.—Anderson was taken sick Thursday and has been out of his head for two days. I got a doctor from town and he says he has a bilious fever and with good care he will come out all right. I've got to like Anderson mighty well and I should feel bad if anything should happen to him. His crazy talk in his delirium was mostly about his wife. I guess they had a flare-up about her extravagance and other foolishness, and that's why he left and what makes him so grumpy about home matters. Poor old Jack has been miserable, licking Anderson's hands and face and whining like a sick baby, and I had to tie him up. The boys around have been very good, offering to set up nights and bringing in quail and squirrels for him, but he has not eaten a morsel. Doctor says to make him some broth. I've managed to get along, but I'm nearly dead for sleep.

Another begging letter from North. I don't see what right he has to ask me for a thousand dollars and without any explanation as to what he wants it for.

CHAPTER IV.

THE FOREST IN AUTUMN—A SLUICE ROBBER AND THE WHIPPING POST—NORTH AS A MONTE DEALER—AN ENCOUNTER WITH A HIGHWAY-MAN—HIGH PRICED HAY—ANOTHER MEET-ING WITH THE FRENCHWOMAN—MEXICANS DISCOVER A BIG BONANZA—AN EVICTION BY FORCE—RECOGNITION OF THE RIGHTS OF FOREIGN MINERS.

A FORTY-NINER

CHAPTER IV.

NOVEMBER 17, 1850.—Pard is all right again, thank the Lord, although not able to work yet. I hired a man to rustle for some chickens and he found three after a two days' hunt. He paid $24 for them and with his horse hire and time they cost me $50, but I don't begrudge it for I made chicken broth and Pard said it went right to the spot. We have had another big storm. It rained three days steady. The grass is coming up, the hill sides are all green and it looks like spring instead of fall. While it is mighty pretty, it isn't like autumn back in old Litchfield where the sumachs and the maples are all ablaze at this time of the year. I worked in the claim alone for three days and cleaned up fourteen ounces. After dividing with Anderson I have got over two thousand dollars on hand and will send it to dad next week. Pard says I would do better to buy land in California, but that's foolishness. The gold will all be dug out after a while, and after that I don't see what there is to stay in this country for.

NOVEMBER 24, 1850.—We both worked this week and took out eighty-nine ounces. When I think of how much money I am making it seems like a dream. I used to work for a dollar a day in haying time, and our hired man on the farm gets twelve dollars a month and found. The regular miners' wages here are eight dollars a day and very few men will hire out. I sent the two thousand dollars to dad and told

him to buy the farm for me, so whatever happens I will have that, but the more I think of it the less I feel like running it. I don't suppose I could make more than five hundred dollars a year off of it at the best, and then have to work four times as hard as I do here, but then this is not going to last always. We caught an Indian cleaning up our riffle box Saturday night. When the miners found out about it they insisted on his being punished and it was decided to tie him up to a tree and give him fifty lashes on the bare back. Nobody would volunteer to do the whipping, so we drew lots and Dick Stiles got the job. He used a double half-inch rope, but the Indian after the first half-dozen strokes made such a howl that we let him go, although there was not a red mark on his back.

DECEMBER 1, 1850.—Although there was nothing to show it, we observed Thursday as Thanksgiving, as that was the legal day in the States. All we did was to lay off and eat quail stew and dried apple pie. I thought a lot about the old folks and would like to have been home with them, and I guess I will be next year, although Slocum's farm doesn't seem to be as enticing as it was when I first started out to buy it. Dad writes that Hetty blames me for not looking up her brother, who don't write any letters home. I think she is unreasonable. I didn't take any contract to look out for him and he is as old as I am. Pard and I talked it over and he says why not take a holiday and a trip to Sacramento, and then I can decide what to do. We worked four days and cleaned up forty-one ounces.

DECEMBER 22, 1850.—This is the first I have written in three weeks. I've been to Sacramento. Pard insisted on my going; said that after nursing him through his sickness I needed a rest, so I bought a mustang and saddle, paid sixty dollars for the horse and seventy-five for the saddle and bridle.

A FORTY-NINER

Sacramento is the liveliest place I ever saw. There are over five thousand people living there, mostly in tents, and not more than a dozen wooden houses in the place. Hundreds of people from San Francisco are coming up the river every day, and the bank is piled up with all sorts of goods and provisions for the mines. About every tent is a gambling house and it made my head swim to see the money flying around. I had a big job hunting up North and then only found him by accident. I was almost sorry that I came across him, for I discovered that he had turned sport and was dealing "monte." He pretended to be very glad to see me and then let out that what he wanted the money for was to start a game of his own, sure that he could win a fortune. Gracious, what would Hetty and his folks say if they knew he had become a gambler. He got very chilly when I wouldn't let him have the dust, but made me promise that I would not write anything home about it. He is living with a Mexican girl and I don't think they are married.

I thought a lot about Pard while I was away. We were strangers a few months ago, and now I couldn't love an own brother any better. He was just as glad to see me as I was to see him, and Jack pretended he was overjoyed. The old dog is so fat he can hardly toddle and with Pard petting him he certainly has a good time. Pard took out of the claim one hundred and twenty-two ounces while I was gone and insists on sharing it, and I could not argue him out of it. He is mighty set when he wants to be.

Jim McCord, who lives about half a mile down the creek, was held up by robbers on the divide about a week ago while on his way back from town. He showed fight and one of the highwaymen shot him in the knee, shattering the bone. Dr. Hunt has been attending him and says mortification has set in and his leg will have to be cut off. That's pretty rough on Jim.

The widow who married the young fellow at Selby Flat has shook him and come back to the Flat again. She says he was "no account," but the boys think he was glad to get rid of her.

DECEMBER 29, 1850.—We decided to keep the horse, as it would be handy to ride to town and over the country. Green feed is plenty, but no oats or grain to be had for love or money. We had to have some feed in case of snow, so Christmas day I rode down to Centerville and found a man who had cut some wild oats in a valley below that town. He wanted two hundred and fifty dollars a ton and fifty dollars more for delivering it on Rock Creek, and I bought it at that figure. That would cause dad to hold up his hands, but then they don't make thirty dollars a day on an average in old Connecticut.

While at Centerville I hunted up the pretty Frenchwoman. She knew me and asked where I had been and what game I was running. I could hardly make her believe that I was a miner and not a sport. Her pretty French accent was very fascinating. She says she is coming back to Nevada in a little while and then she will ride over to the claim some day. I don't believe she will, but if she does it will cause a sensation on the creek.

The doctor cut off McCord's leg the day before Christmas and he died the next day. We buried him on the hill alongside of Donovan. He had one thousand two hundred dollars in dust, which we sent to his wife, who lives in New York City. It was pitiful to hear him mourn about her and his children before he died.

(Jackson's figures are verified on the authority of one Johnson, who, in 1851, sold ten tons of hay, which he had cut on a tract of land he had settled on in Penn Valley, at two hundred and fifty dollars a ton, delivered at Rough and Ready, a distance of four miles.)

A FORTY-NINER

Only worked three days this week and took out fifteen ounces and a half. Our claim is as rich as those over on Brush Creek, and that ground has been considered the best of any around this section. There are lots of miners tramping over the country from one locality to another and we hear stories of the big yield of gold everywhere in the foothills. I have talked with men from Mariposa and Tuolumne Counties who claim to have left ounce diggings because they had heard of better places North. It is strange what a restless, discontented lot of gold seekers roam around from one county to another. They can't make money fast enough at an ounce a day, but are prospecting for some spot where they can take out a bushel or more of gold in a week, and as there have been plenty of such strikes made it keeps them excited and continually on the tramp. I was chatting yesterday with a miner from Mariposa County and he was telling me of the discovery at a camp called Bear Valley that had set the country wild. It seems there are a lot more Mexicans in that part of the State than here and they do a good deal of mining. It was noticed that for a couple of weeks the "greasers" had been very flush, selling lots of dust at the store and playing "monte" for high stakes. Some of the miners put a watch on them and found them panning on a flat about a mile from the town, and they soon found out that the Mexicans had struck the biggest kind of a deposit. It made them mad to think that a lot of "greasers" were getting the benefit of it, so they organized a company and drove them away by threats and force and then worked the ground themselves. Out of a space forty feet square they took out two hundred and ten thousand dollars and that was the end of it; just a big pocket of gold mixed in the rocks, specimen gold he said, that is, jagged and rough and not rolled and water-worn as the dust is in the creeks and ravines. It was an outrage on the Mexicans, but the jumpers justified their action on the ground that California had been

ceded to the United States, and that white men had superior rights to the mines. Anyway, they got away with the gold.

JANUARY 5, 1851.—Another year and I have been away from the States twelve months. I was desperately homesick for a while, but since Anderson and me became partners I am fairly well reconciled, although at times I long to see the old folks. I have not done so badly, for I have sent father four thousand five hundred dollars, have about a thousand dollars on hand and we have been offered and refused ten thousand dollars for the claim. We will probably work it out in three or four months and then hunt another one. Pard still wants to go to river mining, and maybe we will. We had another big week working up the center of the claim and cleaned up ninety-seven ounces. If it only holds out I will soon be a rich man. Our neighbors have finished the ditch and it is over a mile long. We share the water, each using it for one day, and as it carries twice as much water as when we first dug it, there is enough to sluice off top dirt and keep us five days cleaning up the gravel and bed-rock. Kellogg, of Brush Creek, has started to cut a ditch taking the water out of the creek a mile above us, but we have notified him that he must not interfere with the amount we want in our ditch. We do not propose to allow the water to be taken to another creek to our injury.

JANUARY 12, 1851.—It's been raining all the week and the creeks are running bank-full. Over on Deer Creek it drove all the miners out and filled their claims with rock and gravel. They have struck the richest kind of diggings up on Nigger Hill above Nevada, in deep ground, and they have to coyote to get the dirt. They say that they are making a hundred dollars a day to the man. A dozen Frenchmen own one of the richest of the claims, and a party of roughs drove them out

and jumped the ground on the pretext that the French-men were not American citizens and could not legally hold mining claims. There was a big excitement and a miners' meeting called, which decided that the Frenchmen's titles were as good as anybody else's and so the foreigners got the ground again, which shows that we have more regard for other people's rights than the Mariposa miners. We got our hay over last week, but the fellow swore he would not deliver another ton for five hundred dollars. I don't blame him, as there was no road farther than Selby Flat, but we cut away the brush and helped him to get through. Selby Flat is getting to be quite a place. Three families, who came across the plains from Missouri and Illinois, have settled there in the last month. One of the "Pikes" has two daughters, so that there are now seven women on the flat and they talk about giving a dance there next week.

We had a poor week on the claim. Only took out eleven ounces. The pay seems to be in a streak about four feet wide up the center; still, eleven ounces is not so bad after all. I get the nicest letters from home; think I may go back in the spring. I sent dad a thousand dollars for himself and told him I did not want him nor mother to work hard any more. Wrote him to get a hired girl for her and if he bought the Slocum farm to just lay back and boss the two. We can stand hired men at twelve dollars a month. Some of the claims down below us are doing very well, but none are paying as much as ours.

(NOTE.—Coyoting was a local descriptive term of a mining method which meant the sinking of shafts, and running small drifts from the bottom in the bed-rock in all directions until the excavated banks become dangerous, when the shaft would be abandoned and another sunk close by. It was dangerous work and many a miner lost his life by caving banks. It was the direct precursor of regular drift mining, when the tunnels were systematically timbered.)

CHAPTER V.

WEATHER CONTRASTS—ANTICIPATING THE EX-
HAUSTION OF THE PLACERS—A LIVELY
DANCE AT SELBY FLAT—THE FIGHT BE-
TWEEN THE JACKASS AND THE FEROCIOUS
BEAR—DECAMPING SHOWMEN—THE TOWN
CELEBRATES THE EVENT—A FOOTHILL DIT-
TY—THE MURDER OF HENRY NORTH—FOL-
LOWING THE CHANNELS UNDER THE MOUN-
TAIN—THE GROWTH OF NEVADA CITY.

A FORTY-NINER

CHAPTER V.

JANUARY 19, 1851.—Have not written much about Pard lately, but he is a great comfort. He is a different man than when we joined fortunes, doesn't sulk and get moods as he did at first, and I notice he doesn't tear up his letters any more. He says it is all on account of our dog Jack who came along just at the right time, but that is all nonsense, although it is wonderful how much they think of each other. The rain is over, the nights are cold and frosty, but the grass is growing and wild flowers are blooming. When I think of the old Norfolk place, which at this time of the year is buried under big snowdrifts, I don't feel as if I cared to leave this country. It seems a pity that when it is all worked out there will be nothing to stay for. Pard has a different opinion. He predicts that they will grow wheat and fruit in the valleys and California will be a rich and big State, and he tells me that he is thinking of investing five thousand dollars in real estate at the Bay. The claim paid eighteen ounces this last week.

JANUARY 26, 1851.—There was a lively time over at Selby Flat Wednesday night. The landlord gave a ball at the hotel. All the women were there—seven of them—and about two hundred men. They had a fiddler—Mart Simonson; one of the best I ever heard. It was great sport for a while, but towards morning some of the men got too much gin aboard and a quarrel started about the right to dance with one of the

45

Missouri girls. Pistols were drawn, the lights put out, at least a hundred shots fired; but, funny enough, only one man was hurt—Sam Creeley, who was hit in the leg. I went out through a window and did not wait to see the finish. It was too exciting for me.

Had a long letter from dad. He has bought the Slocum farm in my name, but now it's mine I would not go back and work on it as I did on the old place under any circumstances. I couldn't content myself. Pard laughs at me and says how about that little song I used to sing:

> "A little farm, a little wife,
> A dozen babies, a happy life."

A foot of snow fell last week, but it soon melted off. Claim still paying well.

FEBRUARY 2, 1851.—The town went clean crazy this afternoon. I would not have believed that white men could have made such fools of themselves if I had not been there. When I was over in Nevada yesterday I saw on the front of Caldwell's store a big poster which said there was going to be a grand fight between a ferocious grizzly bear and the champion fighting jackass of the State, the scrap to take place Sunday afternoon in a valley just beyond the ridge on the trail to Centerville (Grass Valley). The bill claimed that the jack had whipped two bulls and killed a mountain lion in previous fights at Sonora, and was expected to be a fair match for the grizzly. Most everybody thought it was a sell, but we found out that a ring had been built and preparations made for the fight. I was curious to see it and rode down to the valley in the afternoon along with about all the rest of the population.

Sure enough, there was a stockade about forty feet in diameter, made of split pine stakes driven in the ground and

bound together around the top with strips of rawhide. It looked pretty weak to hold a big grizzly, but one of the show-men said the jack would keep the bear too busy for him to think of breaking away, so we concluded to chance it. A large cage held the beast, a trap door opening into the ring, and we could hear the bear growling, although the chinks were stopped up so that nobody could see the prisoner. The fight-ing jackass was hitched to one of the stakes and for looks he didn't show to whip a sick pup, let alone a fierce grizzly; but the boss was willing to take odds in his favor, although no one wanted any bets on the game. A rope about two hundred feet from the ring stretched around the stockade. It cost a dollar to get inside, and as at least two thousand rustled for logs and stumps to stand on and paid the money it was a pret-ty profitable speculation. After waiting an hour or more the crowd grew impatient and yelled for the show to begin, but the boss would not start it until a lot of outsiders, who had climbed trees and were trying to see the fight free had put up the same price as the rest of us, and, as we all thought that was fair, they had to pungle.

The jackass was turned loose and started in nibbling grass as if he were not particularly concerned in the proceedings. Then, after a lot of fiddling around, two men pried open the trap door, and we all held our breaths, expecting to see a grand rush of a ferocious beast and a dead burro. The bear wouldn't come out until they poked him with a pole, and when he finally waddled into the enclosure there was a roar from the crowd that made the woods ring. Instead of a fierce, blood-thirsty grizzly it was only a scared little cinnamon bear that didn't weigh over four hundred or five hundred pounds. He sat on his haunches for a minute, frightened almost to death by the noise and the crowd, and then walked in a friendly way toward his opponent. The donkey wasn't making friends and when the bear got close enough the jackass whirled and gave him a

couple of thundering kicks in the ribs, and then went on eating grass as if bears were nothing to him. The bear picked
himself up, made a break for the fence, went over it in two
jumps and started for the chapparal.

The crowd scattered in every direction, except a few
who banged away at the beast with revolvers, but it got safely
into the brush and that was the last seen of Mr. Bear. Everybody began yelling to hang the showmen, but in the excitement they had taken to their horses, lit out of the country
and there was nothing left but the jackass. A procession was
formed, the animal in the lead, and we all tramped back to
town, shouting, singing and banging away with pistols.
When we reached Caldwell's store the place went mad. The
crowd would drive the burro into a saloon, insist on pledging
him for drinks, then redeem him by taking up a collection for
the bill, and repeat at the next saloon. The town was in for
a grand drunk, but I soon got tired of it and rode home. I
told Pard about it and he remarked that as we could not
make the jackass drink he was the only sensible one in the
outfit. It was a pretty good trick and the fellows cleaned up
at least two thousand dollars and got away with it. I noted
one queer thing and that was the song in which everybody
joined. A half dozen would sing the verse:

"There was an old woman, had three sons,
　　　Joshua, James and John.
Josh was hung, James was drowned,
And John was lost and never was found.
And that was the end of the three sons,
　　　Joshua, James and John."

Then the crowd shouted out the chorus, which was:

"John I. Sherwood, he's a going home."

A FORTY-NINER

Nobody seemed to know who Sherwood was, or why he was going home. Pard says he heard the same song and chorus over at Hangtown and Spanish Dry Diggings before he came here.

Prices of all sorts of grub are down one-half of what they were six months ago and everything is getting pretty reasonable. Flour is only eight dollars a sack, pork and bacon twenty-five cents a pound, and tobacco retails at fifty cents a plug.

The claim is still holding out well; we have taken out one hundred and twenty-one ounces in two weeks. It is the best anywhere around Rock Creek, but our ditch partners are doing pretty well. I hope to clean up about ten thousand dollars beside what I have sent home; then I shall be pretty well fixed.

FEBRUARY 9, 1851.—I have had a shock this week that has made me feel bad. Wednesday the expressman brought me a letter and a package from Sacramento, addressed to me. The letter was signed Brant Phillips and said that Henry North had been stabbed and killed in a gambling house last Tuesday night in a row with a Mexican. He lived only a few hours after being stabbed, and had asked that I should be written to as I knew his folks. The Mexican has escaped and they had buried North outside the town. There were no letters or papers and he had no money or property except the ivory-handled pistol which Phillips sent along in a package with the letter. It makes me feel grieved and conscience smitten, as it seems as if I ought to have persuaded him to come here. Pard says I am not to blame, that he was just one of the weak kind that was bound to go wrong and I could not have influenced him any different if I had had the chance. After talking it over we agreed it was best not to write the truth, as it would do no good and make his folks feel worse,

49

so I wrote father that a bank caved on North at Mormon Bar, where he was mining, and to tell his people that the accident caused his death. It would be an awful disgrace in their eyes if the real facts should come out; but I don't see how they can, as nobody knows anything about North except myself.

The claim is still paying well; and to think that Henry might have been alive and sharing in it if he hadn't been so foolish! I want to write to Hetty, but I don't feel capable of telling her a string of lies.

FEBRUARY 16, 1851.—Strong and his two partners made a big strike last week. They are working in the creek bank a quarter of a mile below us and it leaked out that they took out over three thousand dollars in six days. Nobody begrudges them their luck for they are good fellows. The news has brought a lot of miners to the creek, prospecting along the banks, but no more discoveries have been made.

I was over on Selby Flat yesterday afternoon and found that while the bed of Brush Creek is about worked out the lead seems to run into the hill. Several companies are following it, sinking shafts and running drifts, and all getting good returns. Kellogg has taken out over twenty thousand dollars and several others are doing as well. They have got the same kind of diggings on the other side of Sugar Loaf and there is no telling how much gold there is in this country if the channels run into the hills. Pard says we had better follow our streak up past the ditch, as it may develop the same as the Brush Creek leads.

I got a long letter from home and dad says he thinks I ought to be satisfied with what I have made and come home to comfort mother and him. It does not seem as if this was the right sort of a life for a man—no women, no church, nothing of what there was in Norfolk, but then there is a lot in this country that Norfolk hasn't got. One isn't so cramped

and it seems as if there was more room to turn around in. I used to think Squire Battell was the richest man in the world, and he ain't worth more than thirty thousand dollars. If I can go back with that much I would not mind; but I never could settle down again to farm work.

FEBRUARY 23, 1851.—It's been no such winter as '49 and '50. About a quarter as much rain and only a foot of snow, which melted nearly as fast as it fell. The nights are frosty, but the middle of the day is warm and the grass is up six inches. Nevada is getting to be quite a town. There are more than one hundred frame buildings beside a lot of tents and log cabins and they are talking about building a theater. There is another town down the ridge, called Rough and Ready and it's as lively as Nevada. They hung a nigger there last week for stealing. It's a queer thing how well we get along without any courts or law. Over in Nevada the miners have elected an alcalde, but his decisions are not binding, only as they are accepted by the people. Most of the cases are mining disputes and a miners' jury decides these. Stealing is punished by a whipping and banishment. Outside of a few cutting and shooting scrapes among the gamblers there have been no serious crimes, and it is a fact that we are more orderly and better behaved as a rule than the eastern towns from which we came.

CHAPTER VI.

A REAL ESTATE SPECULATION — ENCOUNTER WITH A ROAD AGENT—DISCOVERY OF RICH QUARTZ VEINS AT GRASS VALLEY—A VALUABLE SPECIMEN — MADAME FERRAND VISITS ROCK CREEK — RICH DIGGINGS ON THE NORTH YUBA—GENEROSITY OF THE PIONEERS—THE TWENTY-ONE DEALER'S FORTUNE.

CHAPTER VI.

MARCH 2, 1851.—In the last month we have taken a little over four thousand dollars out of the claim and it will take us considerable longer to work it out than we expected, as the flat seems to pay pretty well all over. I have got over two thousand dollars on hand beside what I have sent home, so that I have made more than my mark; still I am not going to quit as long as it pays as it does now. Pard tells me that with what he had before we joined fortunes and what he has made since, he has over ten thousand dollars. He has not sold any of his dust, but has it buried, nobody knows where but himself. He thinks it is too much money to lie idle and has made up his mind to invest it in San Francisco lots. He wants me to join him in the speculation and argues that some day it will be a big city. I haven't got much faith in it and neither has anybody else to whom I have talked about it; but as I owe to him the most of my good luck I did not feel like refusing, so agreed to put in what I have saved. He says we will make a trip to the Bay in a month or so from now and look over the ground together. One thing is certain. We are all fooled in the quantity of gold there is in this country. We thought a year ago that the rivers, creeks and gulches contained it all, although somewhere there would be found the source of it; an immense deposit of pure gold from which all the dust and nuggets were broken off and washed down the streams. Several parties have hunted for this, but they

haven't come across it yet. We do find that the gold streaks run into the banks and under the hills and, in some places, as at Rough and Ready, on the tops of the ridges, and instead of being played out there are more and richer diggings discovered every day. I would not be surprised if it took three or four years before it will all be worked out.

MARCH 9, 1851.—Rode over into Nevada this morning and loafed around all day. Took dinner at the Hotel de Paris and who should I meet there but my little French girl. She recognized me and apologized for calling me a gambler. Said she had made a lot of money dealing Twenty-One, most of which she had saved and sent back to France; but she was tired of the life and thought she would quit soon and go back to her own country. She asked me a lot about myself, where I was working, and said if I didn't mind she would ride out and see me some day during the week. Of course I replied "Come along"; but I have said very little to Pard about her and I guess he will be surprised if she should come. Still, I don't think there is a chance of her making the trip. This is about as pleasant a day as I have passed since I have been in California. Had quite an adventure on my way home. It was after dark, although the moon was shining, and as I struck into the trail beyond Selby Flat some fellow grabbed the bridle and ordered me to get off the horse. My foot at his side had slipped out of the stirrup. Without thinking I gave him a kick in the head which made him let go. Then I jabbed my heels into the horse and started off at a gallop, but I hadn't gone forty feet away when he turned loose his gun. Luckily he didn't hit me and I was soon out of shooting distance. Pard called me a fool for taking such chances and I guess I was, but I got off all right anyway.

The town is all excitement over the discovery of good inside rocks. Over in Grass Valley (Centerville it seems had

been discarded) they found veins of a white stone which we call quartz and some of it has great masses and leaves of gold mixed in. It is the same sort of rock that most of the pebbles in our gravel is made of and we have found in our claims several of these pebbles that had gold in them. We thought they were curious and had no idea that there were solid streaks of it. I saw one piece in Hamlet Davis' store to-day that had been brought up from Grass Valley. It was as big as my head and all covered over with gold. Davis said there was as much as five hundred dollars in it. There was a big crowd looking at it, discussing its origin, and a great many were of the opinion that this was the source of the gold we had been looking for. Others agreed that if there was much more like it there would be so much gold taken out that it would get to be cheaper than iron.

MARCH 16, 1851.—Sure enough, Madame Ferrand—that's her name—came over to Rock Creek Thursday. We were eating dinner and when I went out and helped her off her horse Pard came near falling off his chair. I introduced her and she began laughing and said her ride had given her an appetite and would we please invite her to dinner. Of course we asked her to eat; it was mighty poor grub: tea, beans, bread and dried apple sauce, but she seemed to like it. She talks fairly good English; but imagine my surprise when Anderson began to jabber away in French to her. I was out of the running and was a little provoked, especially as it was the first I knew that Pard could speak any foreign lingo. She wanted to see us working, so we took her up to the claim and showed her how to pan out dirt. Pard saw to it that she had a rich pan, and with our help she washed out half an ounce. Then she sat on the bank chatting until pretty near sundown, when we went back to the cabin and had supper. She wasn't very complimentary about our shanty. Said she

would come over some day and tidy it up, and Pard whispered to me: "The Lord forbid." I saddled up the horse and rode to town with her. So far as I know she is the first woman that has ever been on Rock Creek. She told me that she had come to California with her husband in '49; that he learned her how to deal Twenty-One. After making a lot of money in San Francisco they went to Sacramento, where he was taken sick and died of cholera. Then she came to Nevada with some Frenchmen and won a lot more money here, but she had got sick of it and refused to deal any more. She had an eighth interest in the French claim at Coyoteville and as soon as she sold that out was going back to France, as with what she and her husband had made she had money enough to live on the rest of her life. I got back to the cabin about ten o'clock. Pard was asleep and Jack didn't make any fuss, so I slipped into bed without waking him up.

MARCH 23, 1851.—I have had to stand a lot of joshing from Pard over the Madame's visit, especially as she has made two more trips out here since last Sunday. Of course, I told him she was only a passing acquaintance and he laughed and said: "She is a fascinating little devil, and if she wants you she will land you sure." That is all nonsense. It is pleasant to talk to a pretty woman, particularly if she is decent. So far as I can learn, nobody has a word to say against her except her gambling, but she is no more to me than I am to her and that is nothing.

It looks as if our flat is going to turn out to be a much bigger claim than we expected. The gravel, which is from two to four feet deep, pays pretty well and there are rich streaks on the bed-rock that pan out big. If it holds out we will have at least four months' more work. We average about forty ounces a week, and at that rate ought to take out eleven or twelve thousand dollars more.

A FORTY-NINER

If we do I will be about fourteen thousand dollars ahead for a little over a year's work. That is more than most of the miners are making, but there are lots of richer diggings. Brush Creek has paid a hundred dollars a day to the man and on Coyote Hill they have taken out as high as two and three thousand dollars a day. A couple of miners came down from the North Fork of the Yuba and brought forty-three thousand dollars with them—a pack mule load. They took it from a bar called Goodyear in less than two months' work. They say there are a lot more claims just as rich. There has been quite a stampede of miners from here. It's a curious thing that our gold is mostly fine, very few nuggets, and the gold from there is coarse. They say there was one piece found which was worth six thousand dollars. As near as we could make out the new diggings are about fifty miles north and farther up in the mountains. There is still a lot of excitement about quartz, although it has simmered down some. A general search has been made for these veins and many found, but, contrary to expectation, the majority have no gold in them or so little that the stone is not worth pounding up.

MARCH 30, 1851.—It is astonishing how many people are coming to California. The hills are crowded with miners and prospectors and we hear good reports everywhere. Dozens pass by our cabin every day, bound for the streams farther up the mountains, and as many more on their way back. It don't seem possible, but it is strange the number of hard luck stories one hears, for there are many who are disgusted with the country and are tramping their way back to San Francisco. There was a big fire in Nevada last week and all of the principal stores, hotels and houses were burned down.

We have had a sad case on the creek. Allen Talbot, who is little more than a boy, has been ailing all winter and has been

struck with paralysis. He is completely helpless and the doctor says the only chance he has is to go to a hospital. He had no money, so we raised a subscription. Pard and I gave a hundred dollars and altogether we raised seven hundred and fifty dollars. The lad was taken away yesterday and it is a question if he ever recovers.

As a rule, considering the exposure and hardships, the most of us are in the best of health. It's a queer sort of life we lead; back-breaking work all day; doing our own cooking and washing; no amusements, except a friendly game of euchre and an occasional trip to town. There is nothing there worth while, except the gambling saloons and the Mexican girls at the fandango house. We long for the company of decent women, and while there are a few scattered around and more coming, still the miners do not get much chance to associate with them. I am looked upon as particularly favored, because Madame Ferrand rides out to the claim to see me, and it is a pleasure to be with her, but that will all end shortly. Pard and I are going to the Bay next week and she is going along, and will leave for France shortly after. She sold her share in the French claim for seven thousand dollars and tells me she has got about forty thousand dollars put away. That is a pretty good stake for a woman. I have learned quite a lot of French and can talk a little to her in her own language.

Sam Carter was bitten by a rattlesnake last week over on Round Mountain. He was out hunting and set down on a log and the snake struck him in the leg. He cut out the bite with his knife, rushed to town and the doctor brought him through all right, but it was a narrow squeak.

Kellogg has finished his ditch to Brush Creek. It is about three miles long. He has agreed not to interfere with us, but there is plenty of water for everybody.

CHAPTER VII.

A TRIP TO SAN FRANCISCO—SPECULATING IN
SANDHILL LOTS — HIGH LIVING — HETTY
BREAKS THE ENGAGEMENT—BACK IN THE
CLAIM — NEVADA COUNTY ORGANIZED —
DRAWING MONEY FROM A GRAVEL BANK—
MORE GOLD DISCOVERIES—THE RESCUE OF A
PARTY OF UNFORTUNATE IMMIGRANTS—THE
"LOST GRAVE."

A FORTY-NINER

CHAPTER VII.

APRIL 6, 1851.—Pard, the Madame and I are off for the Bay to-morrow. It was a question what we would do with our claim, as under mining law a day's work must be done every week to hold it. Finally Tom Gleason and Jack Fisk agreed to strip top dirt for us once a week, we to pay them an ounce apiece a day for their work. They are good friends of ours and will keep the jumpers off. Pard is the leader and the most popular man on the creek and we are not afraid of any of our neighbors, but some outsiders might take a notion to the ground. We live up to our home-made law strictly and it is understood that unless the specified amount of work is done the claim is open to location, even when the tools have been left in it. We have had one case on the creek of a young fellow from Maine, who has been laid up with the rheumatism pretty nearly all winter. He had a good claim and in order to hold it for him the boys have taken turns working it for him, putting in one day a week. We have taken out nearly enough to pay for his grub and now he is back working it himself and doing well.

Pard dug up his dust; it was under the chimney back of the cabin. I gave him two thousand five hundred dollars to go along with it and he has sent it down to the Bay by Freeman & Company's express. He says it will almost break his heart to part with "Jack," but Gleason has promised to take good care of both the dog and the horse. We have engaged seats and paid passage in Bower's stage to Sacramento and will take boat from there down.

THE DIARY OF

APRIL 27, 1851.—Back after a three weeks' trip. We have had a great time and it has been a holiday that both Pard and I have enjoyed. It was like getting back into civilization again, although San Francisco is not the same sort of place as most eastern cities. There is a rush of people going and coming, men from the mines with their pile and men from the States on their way to make it. We lived high while we were there; our meals averaged about two dollars each, but we did not begrudge it after a year's steady diet of pork and beans. The gambling houses were a sight and it was good for sore eyes to see so many well dressed and good looking women. Pard made his investment, buying about twenty fifty-vara lots about half a mile out on the Mission road and six over on North Beach. The madame insisted on putting in some money and took eight fifty-varas at four thousand dollars. I never had less faith in an investment. Our land is nothing but a pile of white sand and, while there is some chance for North Beach to grow, the city will never get out to our Mission lots in a hundred years.

The neighbors were all glad to see us back and Jack went wild. I don't know which was the happiest—Pard or the dog. Nobody had bothered our claims; Gleason and Fisk had kept their contract and we will begin work again to-morrow.

MAY 4, 1851.—Am not in the best of spirits. Things happened at the Bay that I did not tell Pard about and I have got a couple of letters from home that are not pleasant. Father writes that mother's health is failing and advises me to quit and come home. Believes my being there would do her more good than any medicine. If I thought it was anything serious I would go, but while I am doing so well here it does not seem right to drop the chance to make a fortune. Anyway, I will wait until I get another letter. Henry North's death has been a great shock to his folks, but it would be worse if they

64

knew the truth. Hetty wrote me the meanest kind of a letter, blaming me for not looking out for her brother, while it was a fact that I never knew where he was until I hunted him up in Sacramento. His murderer has not been captured. I guess nobody tried very hard, as it was a gambling row anyhow. Hetty throws me over, says she can't trust her happiness to me. That's like a woman, but I don't know but it's for the best and I am not taking her decision very much to heart.

After three weeks' rest mining comes hard for a time, but we are both getting used to it again. We cleaned up the ground that Gleason and Fisk had sluiced off and took out fifty-four and one-half ounces. That more than pays our expenses for the trip.

MAY 10, 1851.—Nevada is all built up again since the fire; better and more substantial than it was before. They have also built a Methodist Church on the hill west of the town and have a regular preacher. It was pleasant to notice eight or ten women in the congregation. The Legislature made a new county and called it Nevada, and an election was held while we were gone to the Bay. Caswell was elected judge and Johnny Gallagher sheriff, so that now we have a regular law outfit. Gallagher has appointed Anderson deputy for Rock Creek district and we have a peace officer here with legal authority. If we get long as peacefully as for the past year, Pard won't be very busy.

Showed Pard Hetty's letter and he said: "Give her time; she don't mean it." He seemed to think I was not worried over it, which is true. I have got nothing to blame myself for and why should I let her play see-saw with me. I answered her letter and told her she was the best judge, and, although she had been very unjust, it was for her to decide. Pard don't know how matters stand between me and my French sweetheart. I have not told him that she wanted me to marry and

go back to France with her and I was almost persuaded to do it, and that she finally decided to make a visit to her home and come back in the fall and then we should come to some agreement. I believe I would have made the jump had it not been for fear of what my folks would say and now I am half sorry that I did not go. She wrote me just before she left on the steamer, but it is in French and I can't read a word of it and am ashamed to ask Pard to translate it.

MAY 18, 1851.—We put in a steady week's work and got forty-one and three-quarters ounces. It's like drawing money out of a bank and we have three months more ahead of us if it all pays. The bed-rock is nearly level, but rises up on both sides of the flat and there is no gravel on the hill. The water has gone down in Deer Creek and the miners are getting back into the bed, but it was pretty well worked out last year and isn't paying very well. The best diggings are up on Nigger Hill and Manzanita Flat and there is another place called Gold Run and a flat at the head of it that is rich. Amos Laird & Co. have most of the flat and I heard that for the past month they have been taking out on an average of one thousand dollars per day. There are three or four companies on the head of Brush Creek that are doing well. They are working ground that is from thirty to fifty feet deep, coyoting and drifting. Kellogg is blasting out a rock cut fifteen or twenty feet through the solid granite to drain the channel. He and his partner have taken out over seventy thousand dollars in the past year. Good diggings have also been found on Shady Creek and Badger Hill and there are four or five hundred miners working in that vicinity. It seems as if there was no end to it; we hear of strikes every day and in every direction and we are sometimes tempted to go prospecting, but our claim is too good to quit just yet. The miners generally agree that one should be content with ounce diggings.

A FORTY-NINER

Early in the week a miner came down from Sailor Ravine and told us that up on the ridge where the emigrant road comes through the mountains a party was camped and were in distress and that he was going into town to get relief for them. Pard, who is always first when aid for the sick or sore is wanted, volunteered to go with him and hurry along the supplies and suggested that I should take the horse, ride up where they were and hearten them up a bit by letting them know that a relief party was coming. I found them camped about eight miles up the ridge and they were certainly in a bad fix. There were three families, men and their wives and five children, one a baby not a month old that had been born on the Humboldt desert. The mother was nothing but skin and bone, a young woman, and she could scarcely walk she was so weak and worn out. It was pitiful to see her cling to and try to nurse the baby, so forlorn that the sight would have melted a heart of stone. The rest of them did not look much better and one, a young girl fourteen years old, was sick to the point of death. They had four yoke of oxen, who were walking skeletons, and, to look at them, it was a miracle that they had succeeded in crossing the mountains, as they were in deep snow all the way until they reached their last camping ground, where they had got out of it and in a place where there was some grass feed for their cattle. Their grub had given out and they did not have enough provisions on hand for another meal. It was one of the saddest plights I ever saw, but I cheered them up and told them they need not worry any more as there would be plenty for them all before sundown. Sure enough, Pard, Lawyer Dunn and Tom Buckner rode into the camp before dark, driving a pack-mule loaded with all kinds of grub. It wasn't long before a good hot meal was prepared; there were willing cooks, and we assured the emigrants that their troubles were over. The poor girl was too sick to eat; in fact, was almost unconscious. Her suffer-

ings were too much for Buckner and he swore he would have a doctor there by midnight, if he had to bind him hand and foot and bring him by main force. Buckner is a good fellow if he is a gambler and we knew he would keep his word. The girl's mother coaxed her to swallow a couple of spoonfuls of brandy—Frank Dunn luckily had brought a flask along—and that seemed to revive her. They all felt better after the meal and we built up a big camp fire and set around it listening to the story of their adventures and hardships until Tom got back. Sure enough, he brought Dr. Hunt along with him, who after examining the girl said that it was a case of exhaustion and prostration for want of proper nourishment and that the brandy we had given her was exactly what she needed. Her father broke down completely and sobbed like a child when the doctor told him there was a chance for her recovery. We left them in good spirits, promising to send them up some more grub the next day. Pard advised them to stay where they were for two or three days, until their oxen recruited, and them to come into town and we would see that they got a fair start. This is a land of plenty, but the snowline and starvation is not very far away. We all thought about the Donner party, and it was a coincidence that not half a mile from where these emigrants were camped was the grave of a young girl who was brought out from Starvation Camp by one of the rescuing parties that went to the relief of the Donners, and who died and was buried on the ridge. A pen of logs has been piled around it and it is known as the "Lost Grave."

CHAPTER VIII.

MURDER ON THE TRAIL—A PURSUING POSSE—
WANTED, A FRENCH DICTIONARY—CARING
FOR THE DISTRESSED IMMIGRANTS—JACK-
SON'S CONFESSION—THE JOLLY CROWD AT
THE SALERATUS RANCH—A MIDNIGHT CON-
CERT AND A ROW—HAYING IN THE MOUN-
TAINS—LETTERS FROM HOME—THE OLD
FOLKS TAKING IT EASY—A PEACE PERSUA-
DER—PARD'S DISPOSITION CHANGES FOR
THE BETTER.

A FORTY-NINER

CHAPTER VIII.

MAY 25, 1851.—On Thursday last a fellow rode up post haste to the claim and inquired if one of us was an officer, and when Pard answered that he was a deputy sheriff the man said he was coming in on the trail from Kanaka Creek and just after crossing the river found two men dead; both shot and evidently murdered that morning as they were not stiff yet. Pard left me to clean up while he went down the creek to summon a posse, and the man went on to town to inform the sheriff. By the time he got back with his men, five beside me, I was ready and we started for the place. When we got to Blue Tent we learned that a party horse-back—two Mexicans and a white man—had been seen before noon skirting the hill and making through the woods for the ridge. It was five o'clock in the afternoon before we got to where the men lay and there was everything to prove that they had been murdered. One was shot through the head and the other three times in the back. They were Americans, and as there were no arms or money on them there was no doubt they had been robbed. The sheriff arrived about dusk, but there was nothing to do except set a watch to guard the bodies from the coyotes and send a man up the trail to find out who the murdered men were. Our party tramped back to the creek tired out, but we were lucky enough on the way to get some grub and coffee from the miners at Blue Tent. We learned a couple of days later that the men were miners from New Orleans Camp; that they had cleaned up about seven thousand dollars between them and were on their way to Nevada and the Bay

71

when they were killed. We buried them down on the bank of the river, as it was impossible to pack their bodies in to town. Pard with my horse is off with the sheriff hunting the murderers and has been away since Friday. I cleaned up yesterday afternoon and got twenty-seven ounces. Have not been able to read my letter yet; tried to get a French dictionary in town and found that books were as scarce as hens' teeth, so had to send to San Francisco for it. Think I will study French. Pard would help me out, but I hardly like to ask him as I do not exactly know how he would look at it. If I can screw up my courage I think I will tell him all about the madame. What with the starving emigrants and the murderers we have had an exciting week.

JUNE 2, 1851.—We are certainly having glorious weather. The days are getting a little warm, but the nights are cool and one, to be comfortable, has to sleep under a blanket. We gather up the fresh pine needles occasionally and renew our mattress filling, and the pine smell is not only very pleasant but also seems to be a regular sleeping tonic. The longer one lives here the more the country grows on one. When I was at San Francisco, where it was foggy, windy and disagreeable, my thoughts turned to the mountains and I longed to get back to Rock Creek again. Pard has his theory about it and in his learned way says the main charm is that we go back to nature, where we belong; throw off our artificial civilization and turn Pagans, and that the closer we get to Mother Earth the more we are in accord with what the Great Cause intended for us. This all may be, but pork and beans get monotonous just the same as having none but the society of men makes one wish for the sight of and companionship with a woman. Still, I am afraid I am getting spoiled for I do not feel as if I could take up again the drudgery and hard work of my old life, and if it was not for the old folks

A FORTY-NINER

I should care very little about going back to New England again.

We heard from our emigrants and they are all right. Two of the men have hired out to the boss of the saw mill on Deer Creek and with the oxen are going to snake logs this summer for the mill. The family with the sick girl came over to Blue Tent and have settled down there. The miners in that vicinity have done everything to make them comfortable and are putting on airs because a white family is living there. The sick girl is well again and as lively as a kitten.

I have made a clean breast of it to Pard and showed him Marie's letter. He read it carefully and before translating it to me said that it was written by a good woman. There was not very much to it and some parts of it made me blush, although it was all very simple and nothing to be ashamed of. Said she was first attracted by my fresh young face and her wonder that anyone so innocent looking could be a gambler, and when she found out her mistake and heard about me buying the crippled dog and packing him home she was interested. There was a lot more and I guess I must have been pretty soft when we were together at the city. I don't believe she will ever come back, but Pard insists that I don't know anything about women, their whims and inclinations, and I can make up my mind that she has come into my life and will not go out without a struggle. The "old boy" was mighty good, did not laugh or make fun of me or Marie, but said I would have to choose between her and Hetty and that I better quit mooning around like a sick calf and when the crisis came make my choice like a man. He does not know that the engagement with Hetty is off. Pard says it is a romance of the pines, although there is nothing very romantic in a hero in a flannel shirt and overalls.

The claim pays regularly and it is almost certain that we will clean up ten or twelve thousand dollars apiece.

THE DIARY OF

JUNE 9, 1851.—After doing our washing yesterday, one flannel shirt and the dishes, and baking a batch of bread in the Dutch oven I went over to Selby Flat. There is a young fellow living there called MacCalkins, who has been to our claim several times until we got pretty well acquainted, and he told me what a jolly crowd he cabins with, what good times they have together and has asked me and Pard to come on a visit some Saturday evening. I coaxed Anderson to go along; said he did not feel like having a stag blowout; rather have a pasear with Jack over on the river, but for me to make the trip and pick up some new friends, it might cure my melancholy. Pard gets sarcastic occasionally about my sweethearts.

Well, I went and stayed until three o'clock Sunday morning and it was a noisy old time if nothing else. There are six young fellows living together in a big log cabin they have built near the flat and all are working on Brush Creek. As I remember their names, there were John Dunn, MacCalkins, Charlie Barker, Henry Shively, Delos Calkins and John Hall. They have christened their cabin Saleratus Ranch and they are certainly the wildest bunch of boys on the creek. Barker had killed a buck down on Myers ravine and they prepared a regular blowout of a supper: Baltimore cove oysters, venison steak, fried potatoes and dried apple dumplings and it was well cooked. After supper we sat under an old oak tree, smoked our pipes and exchanged experiences. They were all doing well on their claims. There was not a foot of Brush Creek that was not rich and, like everybody else, they were working to make their pile and go back to the States. I could see in spite of all their joshing that some of them were lonesome and discontented. After a while they struck up some old songs. Barker had a sweet voice and sang Scotch airs: "The Banks and Braes of Bonnie Doon," "Highland Mary" and "The Auld Wife of Alder Valley." The Calkins' swore these

were too solemn and started a nigger song with the lively chorus:

> Did you ever see a gin sling made out of brandy?
> Johnny am a lingo lay.
> Did you ever see a yaller gal suckin' lasses candy?
> Johnny am a lingo lay.

We joined in until the woods rang. The bottle circulated pretty freely, but I wouldn't drink—I have not tasted liquor since I left home; told stories, some of them pretty rocky, and along about eleven o'clock they proposed to serenade the folks up on Selby Flat. Each one took a gold pan and a stick. That was the band and the boys paraded around the flat singing a lot of verses they had made up. Every miner they could find was routed out of his cabin and it was not long before there was at least a hundred in the crowd, banging on the pans and shouting the chorus:

> On Selby Flat we live in style;
> We'll stay right here till we make our pile.
> We're sure to it after a while,
> Then good-bye to Californy.

Of course, the hotel barroom was doing a great business and some of the men got uproariously drunk. One big fellow by the name of Bob Odell began to pick on me because I would not drink and sneer at me on account of the French girl. By and by he called her a name I couldn't stand and I knocked him head over heels and would have hammered the life out of him had not the boys dragged me off, and that broke up the party. I went back to the cabin, bid them good-bye, went home, woke up Pard and told him about the doings and he advised me to shake Selby Flat. Said they were good fellows, but lack of home ties and restraint made them reckless. I guess he is right—whiskey and deviltry seem to go hand in hand.

Some rich diggings have been struck over on Blue Tent above Illinois bar, where the trail crosses the river. I hear that at Gopher Point they are taking out two and three ounces to the hand. We cleaned up last week forty-two ounces, but we keep it quiet. It's no good blowing your horn when there is nothing to gain.

JUNE 16, 1851.—I did some work last week that brought back old times. We have kept the horse I bought to ride to Sacramento and there is plenty of feed for him now. The hills are covered with grass, but later in the year it all burns up and then we have to provide fodder. There is a clearing up on the mountain of some dozen of acres where the grass grew pretty rank and we concluded we would cut it and stack it for fall and winter use. I had a dickens of a time finding a scythe and rake and had to ride down to a valley below Rough and Ready before I could get them. The owner would not sell, but agreed to loan them for a week provided I would pay ten dollars for their use and deposit thirty dollars for the safe return, which I did. It took Pard and me three days to mow and cure it and we stacked about three tons. Counting two days going and returning the scythe and rake and two men three days' cutting, Pard says our hay stack cost us about six hundred dollars. After all, we don't look at it that way; we both enjoyed the change of work, although it was harder than mining. We certainly do live an irresponsible, free and easy sort of a life. Every day on the claim counts for a hundred dollars, but we don't mind skipping a day, laying off for an afternoon or quitting work sun two hours high. Pard says the claim is a treasure house and it doesn't make any difference whether we draw out our gold in one month or three, as long as we know it is there.

Letters from home came yesterday. Dad says he doesn't blame me for wanting to stay while I am making so much

money. He writes that mother is better and that since I sent the thousand dollars they are playing rich folks. He is bossing the two farms and mother has a hired girl. She has bought a new black silk dress for church and he a new buggy, and that is all they have used of it. Bless them! I suppose they think that is awful extravagant. Hetty has not been to see them but once since she heard of her brother's death, but he thinks she will come out all right. There are wonderful tales going round old Norfolk about my getting rich and half the town is California crazy. I would not have believed a year ago that Hetty's thoughts or actions would be of so little interest to me.

I rode over to Nevada yesterday and bought a revolver from Zeno Davis. I hear that the fellow I had a fight with at Selby Flat has threatened to do me up when he meets me and Pard says that a good pistol is a great peace persuader. I won't hunt any trouble and I won't run from it.

Last week was an off week, but we are going now to put in steady work until we clean up our ground.

JUNE 23, 1851.—We put in good licks all the week and took out thirty-eight ounces. It's astonishing how steadily the claim yields. Another thing that makes it pleasant is the change in Pard's disposition. Instead of moping around and sulking, as he used to, he has brightened up and is as cheerful as a robin. Then he doesn't get into the dumps when he gets letters from home, and they come regularly. He got one last night and after reading it he said: "It may not be so in Hetty's case, but there are instances when absence makes the heart grow fonder." Then he whistled to Jack and they went out under the big pine and had a great romp. He's a good fellow and I suppose some time he will tell me more about his life. I know he went through college and hung out his shingle as a lawyer. He can recite poetry by the yard and quote from

all sorts of books. We both went down on the Yuba River to-day and we have about agreed to try river mining when the water gets low. We will form a company of ten men, each putting in three hundred dollars or more, if necessary. We have got to look around for somebody to whipsaw out a lot of lumber, as we cannot haul any from the mills and it will have to be cut on the river banks near the claims.

CHAPTER IX.

WOMEN ARRIVING IN THE COUNTRY—OUR HERO WRESTLES WITH THE FRENCH LANGUAGE— A WAITER WHO COULD NOT UNDERSTAND HIS NATIVE TONGUE—THE RIVAL FOURTH OF JULY CELEBRATION AT SELBY FLAT— CLOSE TO A LYNCHING BEE—PARD GETS A SURPRISE—FORMING A RIVER MINING COM- PANY—THE SANDHILL SPECULATION PROS- PERS—ANDERSON'S REVELATION.

A FORTY-NINER

CHAPTER IX.

JUNE 30, 1851.—They are going to have a Fourth of July celebration and barbecue at Selby Flat in opposition to Nevada. Half a dozen more families have settled there in the last month. Both of the Missouri girls are married; women can't stay single long in this country. Anderson has been asked to deliver the oration and although he bucked at first he finally accepted. It's astonishing how everybody looks up to Pard: he seems to be a born leader. I hear the Saleratus crowd are going to have a burlesque entertainment in the evening. Pard asked me to spend the day in Nevada, as if I would consent to stay away and he making a speech. He is afraid I will have trouble with Odell. Delos Calkins was over here last week and said the fellow was only a big bully and that the ranch would stay with me. I told him I would look out for No. One and did not need any backers, although, of course, I was pleased that they sided with me.

Another letter from Marie. Pard read it for me, although I have been studying French with his aid, an Ollendorf grammar and French dictionary. If any one should hear us around the cabin he would think we had both gone crazy. Of all the fool questions and answers that grammar takes the prize. Pard asks me in French if "I have the tree of my Uncle's garden?" and I say "No, *Jai ne pas;* but I have the rosebush of my cousin," and we keep up this lingo for an hour. I don't believe I will ever learn to speak it. I thought I was getting along fine and a couple of Sundays ago I went into the Hotel de Paris at Nevada. I told the French waiter what I wanted

for dinner and in his own language. I repeated it to him twice and them he shrugged his shoulders and said: "I talk ze French and ze Italian and speak of ze English a leetle, but ze Dutch I do not understand." I was so hot that I walked out without my dinner. I told Pard and he said he must have been an *homme de la campagne* and did not catch on to my Parisian accent. I think Pard was joshing me, but he kept a sober face and maybe that was the reason.

Marie says she bought a *chateau*—that's a house—just outside of Paris, but that she is coming back on a visit to California this winter. It makes my heart jump when I think of seeing her again.

JULY 7, 1851.—I have had an exciting time this week. Everybody in the neighborhood went over to Selby Flat for the Fourth. Kellogg read the Declaration of Independence and Pard made one of the best speeches I ever listened to. The crowd went wild over it and I was mighty proud of him. There was at least a thousand people on hand. Along toward evening the barbecue came off, an ox roasted whole and a half a dozen sheep. The Saleratus Ranchers and their friends organized a company called the "Rag, Tag and Bobtail Rangers," dressed up and paraded in the most ridiculous costumes they could invent and marched around the flat, singing, yelling and shouting until they were so hoarse they could not whisper. I was looking on peaceably, not interfering with anybody, when I heard a shot and felt a sting in my shoulder. I whirled around and saw Pard wrestling with Odell. He wrenched a pistol away from him and beat him over the head until he was insensible. Then he ran to me and said: "Boy, are you hurt?" but I wasn't—just a little graze on my collarbone. I never saw anybody quite as excited as Pard until he found out that there was no harm done. The fellow came to by this time and the crowd wanted to hang him, but Pard

A FORTY-NINER

interfered, saying it would be a disgrace to the camp, so they agreed to banish him, giving him twenty-four hours to pack up and leave with penalty of hanging if he ever came back. That was enough Fourth of July for Pard and me and we went back to the creek and I got lectured all the way home about getting into scrapes. I didn't kick back for I knew he was making believe so I wouldn't think he cared much and was trying to hide his real feelings. When we got to the cabin we let Jack out and sat under the tree, the moon shining, the wind sighing through the pine boughs, the dog at our feet, and we got as sentimental as two old maids. He told me what a lonely man he had been until we began cabining together and how luck had turned and fortune had favored him in many ways since then. He looks on me as a sort of younger brother and I am sure I could not like an own brother any better. Jack wagged his tail as if he understood it all, and I enjoyed the evening better than the celebration; but Selby Flat knocked the spots off of Nevada all the same.

JULY 14, 1851.—It was Pard who got a surprise this week. We had a special invitation to come over to Selby Flat Wednesday night and, although Pard did not want to go, a delegation came over for us and we could not very well refuse. We did not know what was up and they would not let on, but when we got there we found a crowd of about a hundred miners gathered at the hotel. Of course, it was drinks all round; you can't do anything in this country without setting 'em up first, and then Henry Shively made a talk. Said that the miners of Brush and Rock Creeks and the residents of Selby Flat were proud of the fact that they had a man among them who, as an orator, laid over anything that the town of Nevada could produce as was demonstrated by his Fourth of July speech and that the Nevada City lawyers were not to be mentioned in the same class as Anderson. Then he

produced a big gold watch that weighed about a pound and presented it to Pard as a token of the boys' appreciation. Pard was so taken back that for a while he couldn't speak, but he finally caught on and gave them a nice talk. Then he set up the drinks again and we left for the cabin. When we got there we looked over the watch by candle light; it certainly was a stunner and must have cost three or four hundred dollars. There was an inscription:

> "Presented to L. T. Anderson, July Fourth,
> 1851, by his admiring friends and miners
> of Brush and Rock Creeks. He made the
> eagle scream."

For some reason Pard did not seem to be very chirrupy and when I asked him what ailed him he said: "Alf, I've been playing it pretty low down on you boys. My name ain't Anderson and I never can wear this watch where I am known."

I nearly fell off the bench, but he kept on talking: "There is nothing wrong, Alf; I am as straight as a shoe string. There were reasons that when I came here made me change my name, but matters are coming out different than I expected and it won't be long before I will be the man I was before I left Syracuse. When the right time comes I will tell you the whole story and you will not be ashamed of your pard."

Then, as usual, when he got to feeling off, he whistled to the dog and they went out into the dark. You could have knocked me down with a feather, but I had sense enough not to follow. It's a puzzle, but I'll bet my pile there is nothing wrong about Pard.

JULY 20, 1851.—We formed our river company; eight of us, and we let a contract to a couple of Maine men to whipsaw out twenty thousand feet of lumber at one hundred dollars per thousand. Pard is engineering the scheme and says that

about the last of August it will be low water and then we will do some lively work wingdamming the stream. He is sure that the bed of the river will pay big if we can get at it and stay in it long enough to clean up a good sized strip of it. I don't know a thing about it except that it does seem reasonable that with gold all along the banks and in every creek and gulch that runs into it the gold ought to find its way into the trough of the river. That's the way it is along Deer Creek, and we were told by some miners who came down from the North Yuba, which seems to be a branch of our river, that in the fall of '50 they managed to get into it in a half-dozen places and that two or three of the companies cleaned up fortunes. One thing sure, all our old theories about gold don't amount to much. Instead of the deposits petering out, the miners are striking it richer in every direction and in places where we did not think of looking for it a year ago. On Selby Hill there is a deep channel running into the mountain and there is more gold in it than there was on Brush Creek. On the other side of Sugar Loaf, way up on the hill, there is another big streak that seems to run in the same direction as Deer Creek, only it is five hundred feet higher up. Then down at Grass Valley they are taking out chunks of gold from quartz. Since this discovery the miners have got it into their heads that these rocks are the most likely source of the gold and some parties have built a crushing machine which pounds up the rock and leaves the gold free to catch in sluices.

JULY 26, 1851.—Our claim is pretty nearly played out. There may be a month's more work, but the bed-rock raises up on each side of the flat along the hill and there is no gravel in that direction. Pard thinks we had better work together for a couple of weeks and then he will go down on the river to get things ready, leaving me to clean up. If we take out three thousand dollars more I will have made altogether twelve

thousand dollars, counting what I have sent home and invested with Pard at the Bay. He got a letter from John Perry, his agent who is looking after the lots, and he tells him he can double his money if he wants to sell, but Pard says: "Let's hold on and make a big stake or nothing." One night last week after supper, we were sitting out under the old tree, when he spoke up suddenly and said: "Alf, there is no reason why I should not tell you part of my story and my real name. I am not ashamed of it and there is no reason why I should conceal it." Then he went on to say that his true name was————— —————and that he was born at Syracuse, went through college, studied law and practiced in his own town until he came here. He did not build up much of a business and while he was as poor as Job's off ox he married a girl who had considerable money in her own right. He loved her dearly, but she was extravagant, fond of society and luxury, which he could not afford from his own income, and she would not settle down until he could make his way. Then they began quarreling and she nagged him about her money and her family until he could not stand it any longer and, the gold fever breaking out, he left for California. He had made up his mind never to go back until he had as much money as his wife, and, if he failed, why then he would disappear for good. She thought he was in San Francisco, wrote to him there and the letters were forwarded by a friend to Nevada. For some time past she has been coaxing him to return or let her come here,

(NOTE.—While Jackson's frank revelations concerning himself, his experiences, loves and adventures can with safety be given to the world, as he and his kin have vanished into the unknown, the name that he reveals as the rightful one of his partner is another matter. It is that of one who stood among the foremost at the San Francisco Bar and high in the councils of the State; famous and successful as a pleader in many of the noted cases before the courts, an orator of persuasive eloquence and, withal, a man of fortune. He has been dead many years, but his immediate descendants are living in California enjoying the fruits of his wealth and the benefits of his honorable name. While there is nothing disgraceful in the episode, still it is a chapter in his domestic affairs in which the hero must remain unidentified.)

and he had promised to go to the States next spring. That is all there was to the story. He did not say much about what she was writing, but I knew from the change in him that things were different from what they were when I first met him, and he was pretty happy over it. Of course, he would have to keep the name of Anderson until he left Nevada, as he could not explain the situation to anyone but me. I can see now why he used to be so sarcastic about the troubles women could make. I hope it will come out all right.

CHAPTER X.

FASCINATION OF THE SIERRA FOOTHILLS—AN IDEAL FRIENDSHIP—LOUSY LEVEL—JACK AND THE MOUNTAIN LION—THE BURNING PINE—SAWMILL INVASION OF THE FORESTS —MOUNTING A BRONCHO—CRUEL PUNISHMENT DEALT TO PETTY THIEVES—DEPARTURE FOR THE RIVER.

A FORTY-NINER

CHAPTER X.

AUGUST 4, 1851.—What a funny kind of life this is. While I think it all over it seems as if I was dreaming and must soon wake up. And yet the old life in the Connecticut hills is as far away and vague as if it were on another planet. Then I was content to jog along on the farm working from sunrise to dark for eight months in the year and usually snowed up for the other four months. To be sure, we had our fun, the singing school, the sleigh rides, the husking bee, skating on Norfolk pond and I was pretty well content, but I could not stand it now; it looks dull beside what I have gone through since I have been here. If it was not for dad and mother I don't believe I should care to go back. Now I am easily worth ten thousand dollars and perhaps more, which two years ago would have seemed to be a pile of money, but it doesn't look very big to me now I have got it. Not that I do not have to work hard, but the harness does not gall me as it used to. The country is not more beautiful than the Litchfield hills; it is all burned up, dry and dusty, our grub is bad and our cooking worse, but when night comes round and we have had our wash and supper and go out under the big tree, Pard and I smoking our pipes, Jack nosing around and answering the bark of the coyote or sprawled out at our feet, cocking his ears at our talk, the wind singing through the pine trees, the frogs croaking in the creek, it seems as if only one thing was wanted to make it perfect—a good woman for a companion to enjoy it

with you. Pard says: "You remember what happened when Eve came into Paradise? She would make you move into town, put on store clothes and wear a collar. You could not get her to sit out under the tree for fear of snakes." Then he laughed and said: "Make the most of it—it won't last forever." It would puzzle anyone if they should overhear us. We talk in French until my jaws get twisted, and then we plan what we are going to do in the future. Pard is going to the Bay and will open a law office and I don't know what I will drift into. He says that in later years he will meet me on the Paris Boulevards and that I will be so Frenchified that he will not know me. That's all fancy, although it is not so bad a prospect if things turn out as I would like.

(NOTE.—The reader who has followed Jackson and his communings critically will note a change both in his style and thought. The insidious climatic influence of the Sierra foothills is working in his veins. A New England future becomes more and more impossible, and it is safe to predict that his old home will never claim him again, except as a visitor. Romance has come into his life through his association with the Frenchwoman. Although he hesitates to acknowledge it to himself, there is no question that he is infatuated and poor Hetty is out of the running. The fascinating part of the diary is to watch the gradual broadening of the hero, his emergence from the chrysalis state to that of a man of the world. This no doubt was due to Anderson's influence. Pard was an educated man, whose after career proved his exceptional brain power and gifts. He found Jackson in a plastic state and moulded him after his own pattern. Their companionship banished the old note of homesickness and unrest; stimulated Jackson's dormant, but by no means limited, abilities, and totally unfitted him for a return to the Puritanical environments of his old home. It will also be noticed that the diary is taking on a literary aspect. At first Jackson was contented to jot down what to him were the most important items, such as the price of provisions; the weekly yield of the claim, the doings of his neighbors and his yearnings for his former surroundings. His style has expanded; his language is more copious; his thoughts take a wider range. There is even a touch of poetry in his divagations. He notes the music of the wind in the pines; the dog's answering bark to the coyote; the peaceful night, under the shadows of the bough, and, above all, the wonderful friendship between himself and Anderson; that tie of "Partners" surpassing in tenacity and loyalty the love of brothers. What old pioneer who does not recall many instances of similar loyal and loving relations between those who jointly occupied the log cabin, shared the common purse, worked together in the old claim and ate their pork and beans in dyspeptic harmony. I trust the reader will pardon the digression, but the psychological study of the growing of a human soul, as evidenced in these yellow and worn pages, has been of absorbing and intense interest to the compiler and I believe will be the same to the thoughtful reader.)

A FORTY-NINER

Pard is snoring in bed, with Jack curled up on the foot of the bunk, and it is time to turn in. I am writing a lot more in this diary than when I started it and saying things I would not care to have everybody read. I think I will burn it up soon, although I like to go over it and see how it all happened.

AUGUST 10, 1851.—Pard is spending his days down on the river, and as it is only about four miles he rides over and back, morning and evening. I have not paid much attention to it as it seems to me it is going to be a hard job, but Pard has figured it all out from ideas of his own and hints that he has picked up from the fellows who did the same sort of work last fall up on the North Fork. He broke out laughing at supper last night, and when I asked him what made him so good natured he said: "What do you think they call the bar below our claims on the river—'The Lousy Level.'" There are some pretty rough names to the gulches and flats around here, but that is the worst of all of them. The bar is really a flat and about a dozen men are working on it, all doing well. The river is very low now, and Pard thinks we will be able to get into it in a couple of weeks. He will take down five men to-morrow and begin to lay out the work. We pay these men ten dollars a day. We will not have to build any cabins, brush shanties will do, as we will have to quit at the first storm. I ordered a bill of grub at Caldwell's yesterday, about two hundred and fifty dollars' worth, which will be packed down this week, beside sledge hammers, nails, saw and some other tools. There will only be four of the company to lend a hand, as the rest are doing too well on their creek claims to leave them for the river, so we will hire eight men to help us, if we can get them. It's lonesome working alone, although I have Jack for company, as Pard won't let the dog go to the river—it's too long a tramp. Jack had a narrow escape Friday. I heard him barking furiously up the gulch above the ditch and went to

see what the trouble was. It was lucky I did, for I heard a spitting and snarling up in an old oak tree and there on a limb was a big mountain lion, lashing his tail and getting ready for a spring. I think he heard me coming, or it would have been good-bye Jack! I banged away at the beast with my six shooter and think I hit him. He jumped from the tree, made for the brush and that was the last of him. Pard saw a she grizzly and two cubs on the river trail last week, but he had not lost any bears and gave her the go-by. Mountain lions are plenty, although this is the first one I have seen. Think I can clean up the rest of the claim this week, and then we have decided to nail up the cabin and go down on the river and stay there until the rains.

AUGUST 18, 1851.—Finished up the old flat and abandoned the claim. Brought the "Tom" and sluice boxes to the cabin. We may want to use them later. I figure out that with the five thousand five hundred dollars I have sent home, the twenty-five hundred dollars invested at the Bay and the dust I have on hand I am worth over eleven thousand dollars, not counting any increase in the Frisco lots. That is doing pretty well for eighteen months' work; still, there is nothing extraordinary about it, as many have made ten times as much. On the other hand, a lot of the boys are just where they started, but in the majority of cases it is by reason of their improvidence rather than bad luck. It is easy come and easy go, and it makes spendthrifts out of the careless, happy-go-lucky fellows.

As Pard don't need me I am going to lay off for a week and loaf. We want another horse, and I will try and pick up a broncho somewhere. Got a long letter from home yesterday, which I answered last night. Mother's health is better and the old folks are taking it easy. I guess it is all up between Hetty and me. Dad says she does not visit them any

more and she is telling everybody that she has given me the mitten. All right, I won't contradict her, and if Marie should come back this fall there won't be any strings on me. If, by any chance, I should marry a Frenchwoman, what a buzz there will be in old Norfolk. A couple of the Saleratus Ranch boys were over to see me this afternoon. They are curious about our river scheme, but have not much faith in it. I hear there are two other companies who are going into the same sort of mining on the river above Rose's Bar. The weather has been blistering hot for the past ten days and the air is full of smoke from mountain fires. The dry needles burn like tinder. An old dead sugar pine over on the mountain caught fire last night, and it was a great sight to see it burn. The flames shot up in the air at least four hundred feet and although it was two miles away I could hear the crackling and roaring plainly. This is a great timber country. There are several kinds of pines, but what they call the sugar pine is the finest of the lot. Some of them are twelve feet in diameter and two hundred and fifty feet high. It seems a pity that there should not be some use for it. There is a sawmill at Grass Valley, which is kept busy turning out lumber for houses for the towns round-about, and what little the miners need for boxes, and another one up on Deer Creek, just started, but it doesn't look as if there was demand enough to keep two of them going. Twenty sawmills could not use up the supply in a thousand years.

AUGUST 25, 1851.—I have lazed around all the week between the cabin and town. I picked up a pretty good mustang in Nevada, paid eighty dollars for him, and the first time I rode him I wished mustangs had never been invented. He bucked me all over Main Street. The town turned out to see the fun and I could hear them yell: "Go it, Yank; go it, bron-

(NOTE.—And yet fifty years have almost deforested the foothills.)

cho!" but I stuck to him until I got up on the trail and then I got off and made a few remarks so hot that they burned up the chapparal. Gracious, my backbone still aches! Queer thing that when I led him up on the flat and got on again he loped off as steady as a plow horse.

While I was in town Thursday the crowd tied up three men to the bridge over Deer Creek and gave them twenty-five lashes apiece, on the bare back, then turned them loose and banished them from the place with a threat to hang them if they came back. All three were petty thieves, who had been caught stealing. I could not help pitying the poor devils. Two of them howled for mercy, but one gritted his teeth and cursed the crowd with every stroke. There were but a few miners there and it would be hard to get together a worse lot of savages than the ones who stood around gloating over the wretches. The chances are that nine out of ten of the lookers-on, if they got their deserts, deserved the same sort of punishment that was being dealt out to the culprits. The trouble is that most of the men are too ready to set themselves up as judges and, swayed by their passions, inflict penalties, even to sentences of death, on insufficient evidence. Only three weeks ago the mob hung a Chilean at Rose's Bar for horse stealing and the next day the horse he was accused of stealing was found in the hills above French Corral.

We have packed our pots, kettles, tin plates and Dutch oven down to the river camp, and I will nail up the old place and join the crowd in the morning. I sort of hate to leave it, although we will come back in the fall when we get through with our new enterprise. Looking back on the year past, I have had a pretty good time on the creek and have been more than lucky. There is no better companion than Pard, we have made money, our neighbors are mostly good fellows and, while it has been hard work and rough living, we have had

A FORTY-NINER

health and appetites that would breed a famine. I have spent the day writing letters, one to Marie and a long one home to the folks. Won't have much time for writing for the next month or two.

·

CHAPTER XI.

FLUMING THE SOUTH YUBA—IN THE BED OF THE STREAM—A PICTURESQUE CAMP—GUARDING THE GOLD DUST—EXTENDING THE REAL ESTATE SPECULATION—JACKSON FORMS THE READING HABIT—THE FASCINATION OF THE "THREE MUSKETEERS"—A REFORMATION AT SELBY FLAT—AN EXPERIMENTAL VEGETABLE GARDEN ON ROCK CREEK—THE BIGGEST POKER GAME TO DATE.

A FORTY-NINER

CHAPTER XI.

OCTOBER 20, 1851.—I certainly have put in six weeks of about as hard work as ever mortal man did, but am through with it and have made some money. It cost us for material, including everything, three thousand dollars, and we paid out four thousand dollars for labor. We took out twenty-nine thousand dollars in twenty-one days' work for fourteen men, or nearly fourteen hundred dollars a day. We worked both day and night, eight men in daylight and six at night. We will divide twenty-two thousand dollars, or about twenty-seven hundred and fifty dollars for each one of the company. That is not bad, but it did not pay as much as the flat on the creek. Pard is disappointed, but I am very well satisfied. It was great work. First we built a flume close up on the north side of the river and about three hundred feet from the head of our claims, five hundred feet long, eight feet wide, and sides three and one-half feet high. We put up a dam diagonally from the head of the claim to the head of the flume, turning all of the water in the river through the flume. Then we built another dam at the foot of the flume to keep the back water out, and that gave us a stretch of five hundred feet of the river bed fairly dry. We ran two Toms and three rockers steady, wheeling dirt to the Toms and using the rockers wherever we found gravel. There were a lot of big boulders on the bed-rock, and it was around these and in the crevices that we got most of the gold. There was one big pot hole that we thought would

be full of dust, but we did not get an ounce out of it. The richest spots were down stream in front of the boulders. We got one pan under a five-ton rock that had fourteen ounces. The most of the gold was fine. The biggest piece we found weighed a little less than an ounce and quite a lot from a dollar to three dollars. At night we built big wood fires and used pitch pine torches to work by and the canon made a pretty picture, lit up by the blaze. On the 14th it began to cloud up and looked like it was storming up in the mountains and on the 15th it rained hard. The river began to raise and we got our tools out and by night the water was coming over the dam. At midnight she was booming, and in the morning it was a rushing torrent and there was no sign of dam, flume or anything else to show where we had been at work, so we broke camp and took the trail for town. We packed the gold in on the old horse with four of us to guard it, and deposited it in Mulford's bank. I was mighty glad when we got it there for it has been a trial ever since we started to take it out, and the more we got, the more worry. Pard took charge of it during the day, slept on top of it—he worked nights—and I did the same at night. There was not much danger, however, as there were fifteen of us, including the cook—a pretty big gang for thieves to tackle. We have agreed to lay off for a couple of weeks, and what we will do then is uncertain. Pard talks of taking a trip to the Bay to be gone about ten days, to look after matters there, and wants me to go along; but I don't believe I will. If he finds things favorable he will buy some more real estate and I am willing to invest some more on his judgment. He tells me many of the coast valleys are settling up with farmers, who are raising hay and grain and are getting big prices for their crops. It may be a good farming country, but it looks pretty uncertain to me where there isn't a particle of moisture for seven months in the year.

A FORTY-NINER

OCTOBER 27, 1851.—The rain has settled the dust and washed off the trees so that they are bright and clean. Sitting in the cabin door and looking out in the woods, one can't help noticing the different shades of green. It is not like our October woods back home, a blaze of color; but all the hues from the almost black of the firs to the almost yellow of the alder and every intermediate shade. It certainly is restful to the eye. The days are perfect and so are the nights, only it grows chill at sunset and I pile up the logs in the big fireplace and enjoy the warmth until bedtime. The mornings are frosty and cold, but the sun soon warms it up. The sunsets at this time of the year are grand, especially on clear days. Just as the sun goes down the whole western sky is a vivid crimson red, and seen through the pine trees it looks as if the world was on fire. Pard went to Frisco early in the week to be gone a fortnight, and I am laying off and having a lazy time until he comes back. We bought a lot of books along during the summer and some pretty solid ones, among them a set of "Chambers' Encyclopedia of English Literature" and a few novels. I have not read very much as I was generally too tired after supper to do anything but sleep, but since Pard went away I started in on the "Three Guardsmen," written by a Frenchman by the name of Dumas. I never realized before how much pleasure there was to be had in reading. There are seven volumes, and I have read them by the firelight until I could not hold my eyes open any longer, and tackled them again after breakfast, lying on my back under the old pine tree, so interested that I forgot when dinner time came around. There are four heroes: Athos, Porthos, Aramis and D'Artagnan, and they surely had most surprising adventures. I like D'Artagnan best, although Porthos is a great fellow. It's wonderful how in reading so interesting a romance one forgets everything around him and lives in another world.

Have ridden over on Brush Creek a couple of times visiting my old acquaintances. They were all busy, and it was pleasant to sit on the bank and watch them work. They are curious about the results of our river mining. It has got round that we took out a hundred thousand dollars and I did not say yes or no, as some of the partners might not want the facts given. Selby Flat is getting to be quite a place. There are at least a couple of dozen women living there. The wives of some of the wildest boys on the creek have come out to join their husbands, and it has sobered them down considerably. Jim Peters was drowned last week. He was a hard worker, but would go on a big spree occasionally. He got full on the Flat at one of the saloons and started for his cabin after dark. He must have stumbled and fallen while crossing the creek for they found him face downward, dead, in less than a foot of water.

Rode over to the river yesterday. The water has gone down and there is no trace of our work left, except the brush shelters on the bank. I hear that the two companies below us did as well, if not better, than us. I have changed my ideas a good deal about this country. I thought a year ago that by this time there would not be any gold left and that the foothills and mountains would be as deserted as they were when we first came. But it isn't so. More and bigger deposits are found every day and there seems to be no end to it. If it keeps on, gold won't be worth much more than lead.

NOVEMBER 4, 1851.—Pard got back yesterday. I did not know him when he struck the cabin. He had shaved his beard all off, except his mustache, and was dressed up in a "biled shirt"—the first I ever saw him wear—and a suit of

(It kept on and has added a billion or more to the world's stock of the precious metal, and, notwithstanding Jackson's fears, it is about as valuable and much harder to get than in the "Fifties.")

black broadcloth, but he soon shed his good clothes and got into woolen shirt and overalls. Jack was as badly fooled as I was and started to eat Pard up until he got a smell of him, and then the old dog went crazy. Pard tells me that he has invested eight thousand dollars more, of which three thousand dollars is for me, if I want it, and that he was offered eighteen thousand dollars clear profit on our first investment, but did not take it as he was satisfied that by next spring he could sell out for from forty to fifty thousand dollars more than we put in. If this is so, I am worth fifteen thousand dollars. We have been planning what we will do this winter, but have not come to any conclusion yet. Pard thinks we had better try the gulch above the ditch and see if the rich streak runs into the hill. It paid up as far as the ditch, but the bank is thirty feet deep and we will have to prospect it by drifting. He has fully made up his mind to go to the Bay to live next spring, and if he leaves I do not think I will stay here. Our neighbor, Platt, who lives in the cabin below us on the creek, has been experimenting this summer with a garden. He enclosed and spaded up about a hundred feet square and planted beans, peas, corn, tomatoes, lettuce, potatoes and melons, and all but the melons turned out fine. He sent us up some string beans and tomatoes some time ago and yesterday, in honor of Pard's return, he brought over a dozen ears of corn, a peck of potatoes and a lot of lettuce. We had a grand feast. It was the first mess of green vegetables we have had on the creek, although there has been some for sale in town. Platt talks about putting in an acre or more next spring, as he believes he can make a lot of money raising garden truck. We can also get a quart of fresh milk occasionally. Scott has taken up a little ranch on the head of the creek and has four cows. He charges a dollar a quart, but it is worth it. I also got a couple of pounds of fresh butter of him last week. It did not taste like the stinking, strong firkin butter brought out from

the States. Grub of all kinds is getting to be pretty reasonable. The storekeepers in town are stocking up for the winter. I counted nine twelve-mule teams unloading yesterday on Main Street. These teams are a sight, from six to eight span of big mules hauling three wagons. They load eight and ten tons, charge forty dollars a ton, and make the round trip from Sacramento to Nevada and return in about a week. The mules are mostly from Kentucky, and I am told that some of the outfits are valued at ten thousand dollars.

Barker was over to see us to-day and told us of a big poker game that has been running at Coyoteville this week. There were four partners in one of the richest claims on the hill and they got to gambling together. They started in playing five dollars ante and passing the buck. Then they raised it to twenty-five dollars ante each, and Jack Breedlove, one of the partners, cleaned out the rest of them, winning twenty-two thousand dollars. Not satisfied with this they staked their interests in the claim, valuing a fourth at ten thousand dollars, and, when the game quit, Zeke Roubier, another of the partners, won back eight thousand dollars and held to his fourth interest. The other two went broke and Breedlove ended by owning three-fourths of the claim and winning fourteen thousand dollars in gold, so that altogether he was thirty-four thousand dollars ahead. He offered his old partners work in the mine at an ounce a day, which they refused, packed their blankets and started out in search of new diggings. They surely were a couple of fools and, as it was a square game, they can only blame themselves. The gamblers over in Nevada City play for high stakes, but this miners' game is said to be the biggest one that has been played anywhere around this section.

CHAPTER XII.

A TRIP TO THE MOUNTAINS—AN EXPERIENCE IN A SIERRA SNOWSTORM—PERILS OF THE NORTH FORK CANON—AN OPPORTUNE FIND OF A DESERTED CABIN—ENTERTAINMENT FOR MAN AND BEAST—THE RETURN TO ROCK CREEK—HOSPITABLE MINERS—DISCOVERY OF THE BIG BLUE LEAD—OPENING THE ANCIENT RIVER CHANNELS.

A FORTY-NINER

CHAPTER XII.

NOVEMBER 11, 1851.—Pard and I have loafed around all the week, not doing much of anything. It rained a couple of days, but has cleared off and is pleasant, although cold, and we keep a fire going in the fireplace about all of the time. Pard suggested that we take a trip off up in the mountains and see what they are like. We have often stood up on the ridge, looked off at the range and snow peaks miles away and agreed that some day we would explore them, but we have been too busy working to spare the time. We are now in the mood and to clinch it Pard bought a jackass from a Mexican in town and brought him over here. We will use him to pack our grub and cooking outfit and we have planned to start to-morrow or next day. Platt will take care of Jack until we get back.

I have had a sober talk with Pard about our futures. I got another letter from Marie—I can talk pretty fair French and read it—and she says she is surely coming back by the first of the year, if not sooner. Pard says he doesn't want me to go wrong and it is time to quit fooling or else take it up seriously. He argues that I have no right to lead her on unless my intentions are honorable. I had to confess that I had made her a partial promise before she went away but did not have much faith in her coming back. Now it all seems like a dream. I never liked another woman as well. She is straight, and I think I am willing to marry her, but what will the old folks say: a foreigner and a Catholic, and I brought up a strict Presbyterian. Norfolk will set me down for a lost sheep. Not

that I care what their opinions or criticisms may be, as I have about made up my mind that I will never go back there except on a visit. To all of which Pard says that I am hit hard—and he thinks by the symptoms that I will make her my wife if all of New England objects and that it is in her favor that she has seen more or less of the world. He says it's proof enough of her feelings if she is willing to come five thousand miles to join me and that she would make me a truer and more agreeable companion than some little, sniffling, narrow-minded Puritan brought up on Calvinistic doctrine and mince pie, predestined to dyspepsia and doctrinal doubting. That is a mean fling at Hetty; but then Pard likes Marie and is prejudiced in her favor. Oh, well, I have got a month or more to decide and I won't worry until the time comes.

DECEMBER 2, 1851.—Back from our trip. Got home Thursday and we were gone eighteen days. It was in the main a pleasant journey, although we had a snowstorm experience that I do not care to repeat. We camped the first night on the ridge above Illinois Bar and then went on to New Orleans Flat and from there to Alleghany and over to La Porte and Port Wine. All of these places were rich and most of them coarse gold camps, and we heard some big stories of the amount of dust the miners were taking out. The richest place we found in our travels was at Goodyear Bar on the North Fork, and the ravine that leads down to it. We were told for a fact that the bed-rock in this ravine was bare for a mile; that the gold lay along it in piles and that it was picked and scooped up without panning or washing. They swear that it yielded over two hundred and fifty thousand dollars; one piece weighing four hundred ounces and a lot more from five up to a hundred ounces. The claims on the bar were only twenty-four feet square, and as high as twenty thousand dollars had been taken out of some of them. That beats Brush

A FORTY-NINER

Creek, although there are claims on Coyote Hill that paid nearly as well. After leaving Goodyear Bar, we went over on to Canon Creek and followed it down past Brandy City diggings to the river. It had been pleasant weather up to that time, but it clouded up after we left Brandy diggings and when we got down to the mouth of the canon it was snowing so hard that we could not see twenty feet ahead of us. We followed up along the north bank to Slate Creek, stumbling along in the snow, which by this time was two feet deep, and nearly lost one of our horses which slipped off the bank. Luckily the brute fell into the river and by hard work we got the animal back on the trail. We were soaking wet and half frozen, and it was almost dark when we reached the mouth of Slate Creek. By good fortune we found a big log cabin on the flat, locked up and nobody home. It was no time to stand on ceremony, so we broke open the door and took possession. I rustled up a lot of wood—there was a dead pine tree close by and some oak logs alongside the cabin—and built a blazing big fire in the fireplace. That was the most comfortable and cheerful blaze I ever experienced. We could not leave the horses and the jack out in the storm, for they would have perished before morning, so we cleared away the truck from one end of the cabin and brought them inside; the shanty was big enough for all of us. Then we rummaged around and found a sack of flour, a bag of corn-meal, some pork and beans of course, and a cannister of tea. Best of all there were two bunks with mattresses filled with dry grass, which we ripped open. We gave the fillings to the animals and they tackled it as if it had been the best of timothy hay. It did seem as if Providence interfered in our behalf. Our pack of provisions was soaked through and without shelter we certainly would have perished in the storm. Instead, we had plenty to eat, a good fire, a tight shanty, roomy enough for us all, and we knew it could not be very far to some inhabited miners' camp.

A wilder night there never was. We were down in the bottom of a deep cañon, at least three thousand feet below the top of the ridge and seemingly completely out of the world. The snow fell in flakes as big as my hand, the wind shrieked and howled and blew in gusts that rocked the cabin, and every once in a while we could hear the crash of a big pine tree blown down by the gust. A dozen times during the night Pard and I fought our way out into the storm, breaking off the dead branches of the pine log for our fire, as we did not dare to let it go out, and then fought our way back again. There was no sleep for us that night, and yet through it all the horses and the jack munched away at their fodder contentedly, not seeming to mind the rumpus a bit. That is the difference between animals and men. We were worried over the prospect and they apparently shifted the responsibility on our shoulders and the tempest had no terrors for them. The storm kept us in all the next day. We confiscated the corn-meal, mixed it with about half flour and made a mash for the animals, which they enjoyed hugely, and I managed to chop off a lot of young alder branches on the creek for them to browse on. There was plenty of grub for Pard and I, but there was a question of how long we would be forced to stay there. We would have given a few ounces to have been back in our old Rock Creek cabin. However, that night the storm let up and the next day the sun was shining bright. We knew that Oregon Creek was not very far away on the south side of the stream, and as it was mined all along its course we would be sure to find help. Pard wrote a note to whoever owned the cabin giving our names, address and why we burst it open, and about nine o'clock we started out. By taking advantage of the bare spots where the wind had blown the snow away and breaking trail through the woods—in places it was four feet deep—we managed by three o'clock in the afternoon to climb out on the top of the ridge. Here again

we were in the biggest kind of luck, for we came out within a quarter of a mile of a station and packers' stopping place where there was plenty for man and beast. We stayed there two days resting up and then left for home and had no more trouble. That day we crossed the Middle Fork and put up at the Ford and the next day traveled through Cherokee, crossing our own river at the north of Rock Creek, and were soon back on our old stamping ground and safe and sound. All in all, we enjoyed the trip. We saw a lot of wild country, some grand scenery, and wherever we went we found men hunting and digging for gold. I guess we stopped at forty cabins on the way: never failed to get an invitation to grub, never were allowed to pay a cent, and I want to put it down right here that bigger hearted, more generous, or more hospitable men than there are in these mountains never lived on earth. Pard says yes—and deeper canons, higher peaks nor wilder tempests cannot be found anywhere else. It makes us both pretty sober when we think of our two nights and a day down on the North Yuba river gorge.

DECEMBER 9, 1851.—Now that we are capitalists I believe we have both grown lazy. At least since we got back from our hard trip to the mountains we have done nothing much beside riding around the country to near-by localities and loafing about the cabin projecting and planning as to what we will do this winter.

One of our friends is working a claim on Gopher Point, just below Blue Tent, which he seems to think is rich. He offered us a quarter interest for $2,000. We rode over to look at it and concluded we did not want to buy. It is different from any other diggings in this part of the country, and is a puzzle to all of the miners. A bed of blue gravel lies about six hundred feet above the river, on a steep side hill, and seems to run into the mountain. All of the gravel down on Rock

and Brush Creeks and on the Nevada side of Sugar Loaf is a loose mixture of quartz pebbles and sand easily washed, but this deposit has neither sand nor quartz and is as hard as a rock. The miners have to use blasting powder to blow it up and then it comes out in great chunks and has to be broken up with sledge hammers before it can be washed. There is no question that it is rich, as we could see the gold sticking to the rocks; but the men are not making very good wages on account of the difficulty of separating the dirt from the cobbles. I remember now that MacCalkins, who went to Walloupa and Gouge Eye last summer when there was an excitement over the discovery of bench claims in that locality, described this same sort of gravel that had been found where Greenhorn Creek cut through it. As that is on the south side of the ridge, it looks as if the streak ran clear through underneath the mountain.

Friday we rode over and along Deer Creek to learn about a new method of mining being done there. The miners put in a long string of sluice boxes, dovetailing into each other with a lot of riffles in the bottom, then shovel all of the dirt in from both sides, forking out the cobbles and stones with a long handled, six-tined fork. A lot of dirt can be handled in this way, and although the creek bed had been worked over before with rockers and Toms, they say they are making more going over it the second time than when it was first mined. Rock Creek has all been worked out and abandoned and if Deer Creek pays to work over it ought to do the same. We decided to try it and will start in next week. First, however, we had to call a miners' meeting and adopt a new

(NOTE.—The Gopher Point miners had struck into the ancient river channel since known as the Blue Lead, now definitely and distinctly located a distance of forty miles from Smartsville on the west, where it debouched into the ocean that then washed the shores of the Sierra Nevada foothills, to Dutch Flat on the southeast, where it had its watershed in the high mountains. At least fifty million dollars in gold have been taken out of this old channel from the many openings along its course.)

A FORTY-NINER

law to the effect that in a creek that had been previously mined, under the old twenty-four foot rule, the ground could be taken up and held in claims of three hundred feet in length and from bank to bank. We located two this morning for ourselves and got Platt, Dixon, McManus and Ames, our neighbors, to take up four more and transfer them to us by purchase, we agreeing to give them one hundred dollars each if the ground paid. That gives us control of eighteen hundred feet. Then the same crowd repeated the deal, so that each one holds fifteen hundred feet and among us we have over a mile of the creek bed.

Another letter from home and I received a box of things that mother made and sent. The dear old mother, what a queer idea she has of the climate out here. There were in the box a dozen pair of thick woolen socks, two pairs of mittens and a heavy worsted comforter. She said she thought they would be useful this winter and that I would like them because she knit them herself. God bless her! Here I am going around in my shirt sleeves. Best of all were daguerreotypes of her and father. She wrote that they had ridden over to Winsted to have them taken and that she wore her new black silk dress. Dad looks as spruce as a banker and mother is a beauty if she is fifty-two years old. Down in the corner of the box was a Bible. She said she knew I had the one she gave me when I came away, but maybe I had thumbed it until it was worn out. I would not tell her for a thousand dollars that I had not opened it for six months. Gracious! how it brought the old farmhouse back to mind. I can see her sitting by the fireplace, the knitting needles flying and she and dad talking about their only son three thousand miles away. Pard was as soft as I over the letter and the box and his eyes filled with tears, although he tried to disguise it by furiously

blowing his nose. I wrote them to-night that no matter what happened I was going to start home in the spring to see them. I have been away nearly two years and can afford to go if I don't make another cent. It is some comfort to think I have made life easier for them.

CHAPTER XIII.

SETTING SLUICE BOXES—PROMISED CHRISTMAS FEAST AT SELBY FLAT—THE FIRST NEWSPAPER ESTABLISHED—HERMIT PLATT TELLS HIS STORY—A PIONEER OVERLAND EXPEDITION ACROSS THE ARID ARIZONA DESERTS—PERILS AND DANGERS OF THE JOURNEY—A WELCOME OASIS—ARRIVAL AT DON WARNER'S RANCH—SAD NEWS AWAITS THE ARGONAUT AT SAN FRANCISCO.

A FORTY-NINER

CHAPTER XIII.

DECEMBER 16, 1851.—We bought enough lumber in town last week to make a dozen sluice boxes and had it hauled out here. There were about five hundred feet and the mill charged twenty-five dollars for it and fifteen dollars extra for delivering. We have got the boxes made and, if it does not storm, will be ready to set them in the creek next week. If it's a wet winter we are not going to do very much, as a steady rain raises the water so that it would wash out our sluices in no time. In the meantime we will drift into the bank at the head of our old claim and see if the rich streak runs into the hill. Our neighbors down the creek have all got pretty fair claims and are doing well. Platt tells us that he and his partner have taken out over five thousand dollars since they started in and they have got considerable ground left.

Henry Shively was over to the cabin last night and brings the news that there is going to be a grand ball at Selby Flat Christmas Eve, and that the landlord of the hotel promises a turkey dinner on Christmas. Henry says that the boys are betting that it will be turkey buzzard, as nobody ever heard of turkey in this country. He wants me to come over to the dance, but I don't think I will. The last ball I went to on the Flat I came away through the window instead of the door and it was altogether too lively for me. Nevada is putting on airs lately. The citizens are figuring on building a brick courthouse and the town has a weekly paper. It is not much of a

newspaper, but we subscribed for a copy at twenty dollars a
year to help it along. There are about thirty families settled
down there and the moral people have got up a petition re-
questing the storekeepers to close on Sundays. That is asking too much, however, as everybody comes to town on that
day to do the week's trading.

DECEMBER 23, 1851.—It has rained more or less all the
week and the water is so high in the creek that there is no
chance to get our sluice boxes in place. Our neighbor at the
next cabin, "Silent Platt," as we call him, stuck a pick in his
foot and has been laid up for a few days. He's a queer stick in
some ways, rarely goes to town or anywhere else except to his
claim, and does but little talking; doesn't seem to be interested
in anything. That's why we call him "Silent Platt." We
were surprised Thursday when he came up to our cabin and
spent the day and evening with us, and then we found out why
he had become almost a hermit. We made him feel at home
and then he told his story. It seems that he was foreman in a
clock factory in New York, making a pretty good living, but
not getting ahead very much, so when the California fever
broke out he and his chum, who worked in the same shop, made
up their minds to seek their fortune together. He was married and had one baby, a little four-year-old girl, and he fixed
it for his wife and child to live with his wife's mother on a
farm she owned near Hartford, Connecticut. He had saved
about five hundred dollars and it took about all of this to outfit himself for the trip. He joined a company of fifty adventurers that was formed in New York City, and instead of coming around the "Horn," as most of these associations did, the
members planned to go to Texas and then overland until they
reached California. They chartered a bark to take them to
Galveston and there outfitted for the journey. Each member
of the party bought two mules, one to ride and one to pack,

together with grub and cooking utensils, and were even foolish enough to pack along picks and shovels and other useless truck, which, however, soon became burdensome and were thrown away. A captain and other officers were selected, and it was agreed that they would all stand together until they reached Southern California. They knew nothing about the country between Texas and California, except by vague report, as there was no road and no white man had ever traveled it, with the exception of a company of United States Dragoons, which had gone through in 1846. They heard stories of long deserts, heat and hostile Indians, but they were all young and adventurous and had gone too far to turn back. They got along all right until they had journeyed through the north of Western Texas, and then their hardships began. From what Platt related, it seems that from there on until they reached this State the whole territory is nothing but a vast, hot, arid region with only here and there a patch of grass and a dried up river bed. They had to make long marches under a burning sun to reach water and forage and, when found, lay for a week to recruit their animals. They were ambushed twice by Indians, nine of the party were killed and two died from the effects of heat and too much mescal that was procured at various Mexican villages. At these places they managed to buy a small stock of corn and beans and finally fell in with the Pima tribe of Indians on the Gila River, who were more than friendly and did all that was possible to help and succor the party. After staying with the tribe for ten days they pushed on for the Colorado River, two Indians going along as guides. Here they had to build rafts to cross and swim the mules, and one of the party was drowned in crossing. The next one hundred and fifty miles were the worst of the journey. They were forced to travel nights, as the sun was too hot in the day time, and they found water in but two places. On the morning of the second day Platt lost his partner. They had not had a

drop to drink for twenty-four hours, but were expecting to find a sink hole which the Indians had told them about, when his partner jumped off his mule and started to run into the desert. He had gone clean crazy. He ran about a mile when he fell and died in a fit. The best they could do was to cover him with a little sand and leave him in his lonely grave. Platt said that long before they saw any indication of water the mules, which had been barely crawling along, pricked up their ears and broke into a lope, and, sure enough, around the turn of a spur of the hills they came to a perfect little oasis, about half an acre of green grass and willow trees and a pool of fresh spring water, fifty feet across and four feet deep. The mules were frantic and rushed into it with their packs and saddles on, drank their fill and then laid down and rolled over and over. They had but little grub left, but they stayed there two days, in order to strengthen up the animals, as this was the first good feed they had had since leaving the Gila River. Here they turned off into the San Jacinto mountains and rode seventy miles to Warner's ranch, where their troubles were over. Platt says that Don Warner was the most hospitable man on earth. The party stayed at the ranch a week, the men

(NOTE.—In simple words, Jackson calls up a graphic picture of an overland journey in which the pioneers encountered hardships and adventures of sufficient interest to fill a volume, and it would be an historical contribution well worth having. There is a striking coincidence corroborating fully Platt's narrative. Singularly enough, the father of the compiler of this diary, a pioneer, was a member of this same party, and, as a boy, the writer has often listened to the relation of the incidents, hair-breadth escapes and sufferings of these pioneer gold hunters. And what splendid courage it illustrates! Plunging into a terra incognita, at that time less known than the interior of Africa, these Argonauts with superb self-confidence and magnificent daring, allured by tales of the "Golden Fleece," undertook the journey with as little hesitation as a Native Son, nowadays, projects a Pullman car trip across the continent. And of such mental and physical make-up was the majority of the "Forty-niners."

The compiler can add to Platt's story that the party did not break up at Los Angeles. Two or three stayed in that town and Platt followed the coast to San Francisco. The majority kept on, crossing into the San Joaquin Valley, through Tejon Pass, finally settling in Mariposa County, the first mining region reached from that direction. What a sturdy lot of old boys they were, these typical American adventurers, and how little the present generation knows of or cares about them.)

and the mules were given all that they could eat and drink, and at the end Warner refused to accept a cent for it. From the ranch they went to Los Angeles, where the party broke up and scattered. The trip consumed six months and eleven days from New York City to Los Angeles.

Here the sad part of Platt's story came in. He was anxious to hear from home and knew that there should be letters for him at San Francisco. He had written from Galveston and San Antonio, but, of course, nothing had reached him on the trip and he hurried on as fast as possible, eager to get the home news before striking for fortune at the mines. The letters were there, all from his mother-in-law. His wife had sickened and died in six weeks after his departure. Platt says that for a week he was out of his mind and that half a dozen times he went down to the wharf, fully determined to jump off and end his misery. Then the memory of his little girl came to him and held him back. After the first acute agony was over he realized that he still had something to live for, and resolving to devote himself to the baby he sold his mules, for which he got four hundred dollars, sent three hundred dollars to the grandmother and started for the mountains. He fell in with Dixon, his partner, on the boat bound for Nevada, and finally settled down on Rock Creek. They had both done well and were in a fair way to be independent. The child was healthy, well taken care of, and he was in hopes in a year or so to bring her and her grandmother to California. He had neither inclination nor desire to see the States again.

CHAPTER XIV.

A SENSATION ON THE FLAT—THE MYSTERIOUS DISAPPEARANCE OF THE TURKEYS—THE NO-GOBBLER BETTORS WIN THEIR WAGERS—AN ANGRY LANDLORD—THE SALERATUS RANCH UNDER SUSPICION—JUST A PLAIN, EVERY-DAY DINNER—THE RENDEZVOUS AND A FEAST DOWN THE CREEK—THE SWEET-HEART DELAYS HER RETURN—THE JACKASS ESCAPES A SERENADE.

A FORTY-NINER

CHAPTER XIV.

DECEMBER 30, 1851.—Selby Flat has had a sensation which has furnished the boys no end of fun. There was no turkey dinner Christmas, that is, at the hotel, although the landlord swears that his birds furnished a private feed to somebody and he is vowing vengeance on those he suspects of depriving his boarders of a grand blowout. The majority were skeptical as to there being any turkeys procurable and they backed their opinions with their money, while a few who were in the secret took all of the bets offered, knowing that the landlord had made arrangements a month previous with a peddler from the valley, who assured him that he was going to bring a load from a flock that had been raised on a ranch below Marysville and had agreed to deliver to him a dozen fat birds. Sure enough, a week before Christmas, he arrived with six coops full—a hundred altogether; had no difficulty in selling them at from eight to ten dollars each, and the landlord got his dozen, as agreed. Those who bet on a turkey dinner wanted to be paid their stakes then and there, but the wagers were on a Christmas feast and the stakeholders decided to wait until that day before giving up the money. It was a sure thing, so no objection was made. The birds were cooped up and stuffed with all they could eat, the landlord advertised the feed at two dollars and a half a head, and was rash enough to promise mice pie for dessert. Two days before Christmas the dreadful word went around that the turkeys had disappeared, and the Flat was all torn up over the news. The landlord was frantic, but had no clue as to the thieves, although he,

as well as everybody else around the Flat, suspected the Saleratus Ranch boys, they being usually at the bottom of any deviltry going on.   He even went so far as to demand that Pard, who is the deputy sheriff, should search their cabin, but Anderson declined unless a search warrant was sworn out, which the landlord, who had nothing to go on beyond his suspicions, could not very well do.   The women pronounced it a shame and the men said it would be unhealthy for the occupants of any cabin near which turkey feathers or bones might be found.

It was just a plain, ordinary dinner at the hotel, except for the mince pie, and was followed by a Christmas dance. After the dinner the guests—about fifty of them—decided that they would pay a visit to the Saleratus Ranch and see what sort of holiday grub the boys were having.   If they expected to find turkey they were badly disappointed, for there was nothing in sight but the regular old pork and beans and boiled beef.   The ranch boys said that they had fully expected to eat a turkey dinner at the hotel, which, of course, was not to be had, so as they had their mouths made up for a taste of the bird, they were all going over to Nevada for supper, as turkey was plenty in that town, and, sure enough, about three o'clock they all started for that place.   After that nobody suspicioned them, and it was the general belief that some thieving Indian from the campooda, over the ridge, had robbed the turkey roost.   I was saddling up my horse to go into town when Charlie Barker came over to the creek and asked me and Pard to meet a lot of the boys down where Brush and Rock Creeks come together, about two miles below Selby Flat.   He was grinning and chuckling over some great joke and wouldn't let on what it was, but teased us to go with him to the rendezvous.   Pard suspected what was up and said that as an officer of the law he guessed he had better stay away, but just for curiosity I went along.   The cabin we were bound for was

A FORTY-NINER

Jack Ristine and Carter's place. The rest of the boys went up the road to Sugar Loaf, as if on the way to Nevada, but instead branched off down the ridge and hill, and when just before dark we reached the shanty, there were about twenty of them gathered there and, shameful to tell, the turkeys were there too. It seems that all of those who had bet on there being no turkey dinner were in a plot. They had stolen the birds, taken them down to the creek, killed and picked them, throwing the feathers into the running water, and then half a dozen, who were not suspected, had slipped away Christmas day and helped Ristine and Carter prepare the feast. It was a bully good supper and I must say I enjoyed it. The boys were full of fun, and as whiskey was more than plenty, they were soon full of that too. They sang and told stories until about eleven o'clock, then gathered up the bones and remnants of the supper, dug a hole in the bank of the creek and buried the remains three feet deep. They all stood around the hole, or grave, as they called it, bareheaded, while Arthur Brooks delivered a funeral oration over the "dear departed." As they were getting uproarious I slipped away and came back home. I told Pard about it and he laughed and said that the boys did not mean any harm but it was just a little rough on the landlord.

JANUARY 6, 1852.—I had a disappointment for my New Year. I have been expecting every day to hear that Marie had got back to San Francisco, but instead I got a letter saying that unless I insisted on her coming at once she would wait a couple of months more before starting for America. She was looking after her investments and visiting her people—she had a mother and two sisters living in Paris—and as she did not know when we would go back together, was staying longer than she planned. The letter gave me a fit of the blues and I almost made up my mind to take a plunge, leave the country

and go to Paris myself. Pard hurt me by jokingly suggesting that some Frenchman had cut me out, and maybe he is right; but if that is true what would be the use of me making the journey for nothing. I wrote her a long letter, telling her that I was in earnest, and if she intended to keep her promise she must come back without delay.

It doesn't look as if we were going to get into the creek very soon with our new mining scheme, as it keeps on raining just enough to raise the water to a flood level. In the meantime we have got tired of loafing and have started to drift on our old claim. It is not paying very big. The streak of pay dirt is only about two feet wide and a foot deep. We have to shore up the ground with timber and it takes us a lot of our time cutting it. We drifted about eight feet last week and took out eleven ounces.

Our jackass is getting to be a nuisance and is almost as much of a pet as Jack, although we don't let him sleep in the cabin, a liberty which, judging by his actions, he seems to think should be allowed him as well as the dog. He gives us a concert in the early morning that wakes up the woods; follows at our heels to the claim; when we visit our neighbors, trots along as if social duties were in his line, and "he-haws" and brays whenever we are out of sight. Pard says that with the exception that he is too fat, he has all the symptoms of being in love.

CHAPTER XV.

STRANGE DISAPPEARANCE OF CARTER AND RIS-
TINE—A DESERTED SHANTY—RISTINE'S
DEATH—REVELATIONS AT THE INQUEST—
WHO STOLE THE TURKEYS?—A RICH STREAK
ON THE BED-ROCK—PARD BARS THE BANJO—
HETTY HAS A CHANGE OF HEART—THE IN-
TERIOR OF A MINER'S CABIN—A SENTIMEN-
TAL PICTURE—FRIENDSHIP, PROSPERITY,
AND CONTENTMENT.

CHAPTER XV.

JANUARY 13, 1852.—The country is stirred up over a mysterious tragedy that nobody seems able to solve. Neither Ristine nor Carter, the two miners at whose cabin we ate our Christmas supper, have been seen by anybody since that night. No attention would have been paid to this, as the boys do not keep track of each other to any extent, had it not been that Sunday, a week ago, Henry Shively went down to their place to pay them a visit. He found the door of the cabin open, and no sign of the men around. This would not have seemed strange had not the inside of the shanty looked as if no one had been there for a week. The fire was dead in the fireplace and a pot of beans that hung on the hook had been there for days, as the contents were sour and mouldy. The flower sack had been gnawed open in places and flour was scattered over the floor—no doubt the work of coyotes and mountain rats. Nothing else seemed to have been disturbed. Shively went down to their claim, which was close by, and found their Tom and tools in place, the picks and shovels and the Tom iron were rusty, proving that they had not worked in the mine for a week or more. Thinking it queer he concluded to come up and tell Pard the circumstances, which he did, meeting Anderson on the trail coming back from town. Pard turned back and went with him to their cabin, taking Platt along. They found everything as Shively had told them, noted that the best clothes were hanging over their beds, a shotgun and rifle on pegs over the fire-

place, and a six-shooter under one of the pillows. On a little shelf by the window, where the gold scales stood, there was a yeast powder can with about five ounces of gold in it. It was certain from the looks of things that the men had no intention of leaving, and it was also sure that they had not been near their cabin or their claim for a week or ten days. Pard came home and told me about it and next morning early we rode down to Selby Flat to see if anything had turned up to explain the mystery. Nobody there had seen anything of the missing men since Christmas. After talking it over it was agreed that a delegation should go over to Nevada and find out if they had been there, or had left by any of the stage lines, while about twenty of us formed a searching party to look the country over in the vicinity of the cabin. In the middle of the forenoon we heard some of the boys shouting up on the hill and, on going to them, found out that they had discovered Ristine's body under a manzanita bush. It was in bad shape and the coyotes had torn off both arms, but the face was not touched. A watch was left, the coroner notified, and that afternoon an inquest was held. Outside of the fact that Ristine was dead, nothing was developed and the jury returned a verdict of "died from unknown causes." Then a thorough search of the cabin was made and inside of the mattresses a big buckskin purse was found, which contained about eight hundred dollars in dust. In a box under the other bunk there were three yeast powder cans that were full to the top with gold. We buried Ristine close to where we found his body and it was a sickening job. From letters in the box it was learned that both men were married. One came from Reading and the other from Pittsburgh, Pennsylvania. There is no suspicion of robbery, for there was nothing stolen, and it doesn't look like murder, for if one had killed the other the murderer would certainly have hidden the traces of his crime and not have left the gold dust behind if he intended to quit

the country. The general opinion is that Carter is dead and that his remains will be found somewhere around.

Even a tragedy generally has its funny side. At the inquest it all came out about the turkey supper, and now the landlord says he will sue the crowd for damages, prosecute them for petty larceny, and the sinners are wondering if he will carry out his threat.

We worked in the drift the rest of the week, but it is not panning out very well. We cleaned up seven ounces, but that is more than grub money, and we will stay with it until we can get into the creek. I bought a banjo when I was over in town Tuesday and am learning to pick it. Pard says that as a nuisance it is a toss up between me and the jackass.

JANUARY 20, 1852.—It rained, snowed, and has been disagreeable weather all week. The drift is slow work, as it takes about half the time to cut timbers and put them in place. Timbering it not a greenhorn's job and we made a poor fist at it until we went over to Coyotesville and took notes of the drift mines there. We struck a rich little streak in the tunnel, not more than three inches wide and right on the bedrock. It looked as if it had been poured out of a bag, it was so regular. We panned it out and as far as we followed it we got an ounce to the pan. Altogether, we took out over twenty ounces. That is like old times.

Pard struck a bargain with me. If I would agree not to practice on the banjo when he was around—I don't see why he don't like it for I can already play "Old Bob Ridley" and "Camptown Girls' pretty well—he would read aloud to me a new novel that he had bought: "Nicholas Nickelby," by an Englishman named Dickens. I had already read his "Pickwick Papers" and it was a great book, so I agreed and the consequence has been that we have not gone to bed a night this week before midnight. Some of the chapters are very funny

and some pathetic, but it is all interesting. I am not very sentimental, but as I stretched out on the bunk listening, the big drops of rain pattering on the roof, the wind whistling through the trees and the firelight flashing on Pard's handsome face, I thought this was a pretty good old world after all, and I was lucky to be in it. Pard's voice was like a lullaby and I got to thinking of Marie and dreaming of the future. Perhaps some day I might see London and Yorkshire and follow D'Artagnan's road through France. Then Pard shut the book with a slam and said I was a lunkhead and he would not read any more to such an unappreciative fellow. He did not know what dream pictures I was conjuring up.

There have been no more discoveries about Ristine and Carter and it seems as if it would always be a mystery.

JANUARY 27, 1852.—It turned out cold and there has been a big snowstorm. The whole country is covered with snow three feet deep. It was a pretty sight, the spruce and fir trees loaded with snow, and when the sun comes out they sparkle like diamonds. It put me in mind of the hemlock woods in old Litchfield.

I got a long letter from Hetty, the first she has written in months, and now I am up a tree. She says that when the news came to her of her brother's death she was nearly crazy with grief and did not realize how harsh a letter she had sent to me. Now she is sorry for it, admits that she has been unjust and if I will forgive her we will forget all about it and be the same to each other that we were before it happened. I wish she had not changed her mind, for I do not have the liking for her that I did when I started for California. Marie is in my mind all day, I dream of her nights and I never can go back to my boyish love. I have not shown Pard the letter yet, and don't think I will. Somehow I am getting so that I do not

like to have him ridicule me. In a great many ways I am a
different man than I was when I left the States. I thought I
was a pretty smart fellow around the old neighborhood, and
was chock full of conceit. Now I can look back and see what a
greenhorn I was in many respects. I had a fair schooling,
for beside the district school house I went three terms to the
academy. After that I worked on the farm steadily until I
started for California. The farthest I was ever away from
home up to that time was to Litchfield, the county seat, sixteen miles. I never read anything but the New York Tribune
and the Litchfield Inquirer, two papers that dad subscribed
for. Mother was dead set against novels and the only books
we had in the house were "Pilgrim's Progress," "Fox's Book
of Martyrs," "Pollock's Course of Time," "Young's Night
Thoughts," "Calvin's Institutes of the Christian Religion,"
"Jonathan Edwards' Sermons," and the Bible, of course.
That was pretty dry stuff and I did not take to it. I knew
less about the world than I did about Heaven, for, from what
I could hear, I had an idea that New York was the biggest city
on earth. I knew better, but that was my narrow way of
thinking. Pard drew a diagram, which he said expressed my
mental and geographical ideas, as follows, and I guess he was
right:

O   O   o
Norfolk. United States. The World.

Well, I have outgrown that, and while I don't set up for
a traveler, or claim much experience, I certainly see everything in a different light. Our old cabin is not much to look
at outside or inside; dad wouldn't keep his hogs in such a
place, yet one could not be more comfortable or more contented than I have been for the past year. I have been lone-

some at times and have had blue spells, but they did not last very long. There is nothing but a dirt floor, which we wet down every day to keep it hard, a couple of bunks filled with pine needles where we roll up in our blankets and on which we sleep like logs; three-legged stools for seats; a plank for a table; an open fireplace five feet wide; an iron kettle and a coffee pot; a Dutch oven and a frying pan to cook in (it used to be tin plates and cups until we got high-toned and bought crockery); grub stored away most anywhere; a shelf full of books—we have bought about fifty volumes altogether—and that is about all. We put a big oak-back log in the fireplace, pile up big chunks in front and the wind can howl, the snow fall and the rain beat on the roof, what do we care? The flames leap up the chimney and light the old cabin, the dog stretches out in front of the fire and grunts with contentment or dreams, for often his legs twitch, he whimpers and barks softly, his eyes closed, then wakes up, looks at us in a foolish way until he realizes his surroundings, and goes to sleep again. Pard grows sentimental and quotes poetry and gets down a book, reads a chapter or two and we are off in our minds to England, France, or Spain (we are reading Irving's "History of Granada"). Then we turn into our bunks, the fire dies down to coals, and as they sputter and sparkle I lie and watch the glow and see all sorts of pictures until my eyelids grow heavy, and I don't know anything more until I get a dig in the ribs and Pard says: "Get up, you lazy whelp, and help get breakfast."

I suppose we are contented because there is nobody to boss us—"Not even a woman," puts in Pard—have money enough so that we need not live this way if we don't want to, no scandal, no gossip, and nobody to criticise us as long as we keep off of other people's corns, a jolly good lot of neighbors who live as we do, and our friendship, which is the thing that counts more than all the rest. Naturally, I don't want to live

this way forever and we have our plans for the future; but in the meantime and until things ripen, we are satisfied with the old cabin.

The snow is so deep that it is difficult to cut timber and we did little work during the week. The rich streak held on for about four feet, and from that and the rest of the gravel we made seventeen and one-half ounces. It has rained or snowed steadily for almost two weeks. We bought a couple of pairs of rubber boots and two tarpaulin coats to tramp between the cabin and the claim. Luckily, we had laid in enough grub to last a month; there is plenty of hay for the horses and the jackass, and they are as fat as butter, so none of us are suffering any hardships.

(NOTE.—Jackson draws a graphic sketch of the miner's life and touches partially on its fascination. Of course, he had his plans for the future, they all had; but in many cases the plans bore no fruition, and the foothills held them to the end.)

CHAPTER XVI.

THE RAGING YUBA—A VISIT TO THE RIVER—BAD CASE OF JIM-JAMS—A SWARM OF TIN JACKETED IMPS—SUNDAY IN NEVADA—FOOD FAMINE IN THE MINING CAMPS—RATTLESNAKE DICK SHOOTS UP THE TOWN—A QUARTZ MINING SPECULATION AND ITS FAILURE.

A FORTY-NINER

CHAPTER XVI.

FEBRUARY 3, 1852.—We had a glimpse or two of the sun last week; but it rained most of the time, carrying off the snow with it. I rode down to the Yuba River yesterday afternoon and it was a sight to see.

The river is more than bank full, all of ten feet deep, and a madder, wilder rush of water was never seen. I could hear the great rocks grinding and crushing against each other as they rolled over and over, big logs and pine trees swirling down the stream or tumbling end over end as they butted against some obstruction, and the noise was deafening. It was a grand sight and did not look much like the place where we mined last fall.

We very nearly had another tragedy on the creek early in the past week. Andy Collins, an Irishman, who has lived alone in his cabin, about a mile below us, for a year or more, has been a hard drinker ever since we have known him. He bought his rum by the gallon and kept soaked all the time. Tuesday night he had a bad attack of the jim-jams, and his nearest neighbor, O'Neil, heard him yelling and shrieking like all possessed. He rushed down, opened the door and found Collins cowering in one corner, striking at imaginary swarms of imps in the air. "Don't you see them?" he yelled; "little devils with tin jackets on. Look at them coming down the chimney and through the window, hundreds of 'em!" With that he rushed through the door, out into the rain and darkness, and O'Neil lost sight of him. He at once roused every-

body up and down the creek, but we might as well have looked for a needle in a hay mow. We kept up the search until one or two o'clock and then quit until daylight. The general opinion was that he had jumped into the creek and had been drowned, as there was four feet of water in it, and running like a mill race. He was not born to be drowned, for we found him next day over on Round Mountain, nearly dead with exposure and cold. It was a job to pack him back, as we had to make a litter to carry him. We got him into his cabin, warmed him up, and when he came to, dosed him with strong tea. He was in his right senses, too, and had forgotten all about his little tin devils. Now we have got to nurse him and sit up with him nights until he gets on his legs again. No whiskey for me. We have never had a drop in the cabin since we have lived here.

It has been a poor week on the claim. While there is plenty of gravel, it is almost barren. All we got for our week's work was a little over an ounce. That isn't even grub wages. Still, we are not as unlucky as we might be.

Anderson received a letter from Perry, our agent, saying that he could sell out our holdings, including North Beach, at an advance of twenty-two thousand dollars. It was a tempting price to me, as I would get in all, with what I put in, over ten thousand dollars. Pard said "No, let's hold on until we clean up fifty thousand dollars." I think he is making a mistake, but I am bound to stay with him, and trust to his judgment.

FEBRUARY 10, 1852.—I spent the day over in Nevada. It is getting to be quite a big town. What a contrast it is to our poky, slow New England villages. There are half a dozen stores which carry all kinds of provisions and hardware, two jewelry shops, two bakeries, a gunsmith store, butcher shop, five hotels, and gin mills too numerous to mention. Saturday

A FORTY-NINER

night and Sundays—I forgot, one church—are the lively days. Then there are two or three thousand miners in town, the majority drinking, gambling and carousing. Woolen shirts and duck overalls are the fashion, and if you see anybody dressed up it's a sure thing he is either a gambler or a lawyer. What beats me is the craze the miners have for gambling. Every saloon has some sort of game running, and the big ones have a dozen. "Monte," "Red and Black," "Chuck-a-luck," "Twenty-one," "Rondo," and "Fortune Wheels," are the banking games, and they play poker and "Brag" for big stakes. The fool miners work hard all the week and then lose their dust at these games of chance. There does not seem to be much chance about them, for nobody ever heard of a miner winning anything. Of course, the miners don't all gamble; in fact, a lot of them do their trading, get a square meal at the hotel, and go back to their claims. Still, enough waste their money to keep the sports slick and fat. I suppose they are looking for excitement—anything to break the monotony—and this is the way they get it.

Charley Donaldson, who had a rich claim on Brush Creek, worked it out last fall and left for the States with six or seven thousand dollars. In a couple of weeks he was back again hunting for new diggings, and it leaked out afterward that he lost every cent in a Frisco gambling hell. I have never tried my luck but once, and then I lost seventy dollars in half an hour. I don't regret it, though, for then it was when I met Marie and it was more than worth the price.

It looks as if it were going to be as wet a season as Fortynine. It has rained or snowed almost every day for a month. Teaming has quit and the stages don't make regular trips. Provisions have jumped up to double prices. Flour is scarce and the storekeepers are asking thirty dollars for a hundred pound sack. Last winter they all put in big stocks. It was a dry season and they lost money. This year they thought they

could team the same as last and did not lay in heavy supplies, and, as a consequence, if the rains don't let up, there is a prospect of a famine. I am told that there are eight big team outfits loaded with flour, stuck in the mud, between here and Sacramento. Rattlesnake Dick, a sport and a desperado from Auburn, was chased out of town last week. He shot up a fandango house, held up a monte bank and then abused Stanton Buckner like a pickpocket, making the old fellow go down on his knees and beg for his life. About this time the citizens began to gather with shotguns and Dick took to his horse and struck out for some other camp. Buckner is a nice old fellow, a lawyer, prides himself on his Kentucky breeding, and swears that nothing but blood will wipe out the insult. I guess he won't hunt Dick very far.

A prospector found what is supposed to be Carter's hat and coat down in Myers Ravine. Outside of that there have been no developments. Some think that Carter is still alive and has left the country, but the majority believe he is dead. It is a strange affair.

We worked a little in the tunnel and found nothing worth while. The weather is too bad to do any prospecting and there is no telling when we can get into the creek. Mining is almost suspended, except where they are drifting and coyoting. At Grass Valley they are working several big quartz veins and it is said that they are very rich. At the Rocky Bar claim over seventy-five thousand dollars have been taken out in the last four months. They have found two or three quartz veins along Deer Creek that pay pretty well, working them by the Mexican arrastra process. A scientific cuss in Nevada has formed a company to get the gold out of the quartz by a new method and is selling shares like hot cakes at ten dollars a share. He is going to build a furnace and melt the gold out of the rock. It may be all right, but I don't know anything about quartz mines and have not bought any

A FORTY-NINER

stock. I hear, as a rule, miners have fought shy of the investment, as the majority are skeptical and don't believe in any new-fangled process for getting gold out of rocks, but the business men don't feel that way. I am told that the merchants, lawyers and a great many sporting men have put money into the scheme and the inventor has raised about forty thousand dollars. He is grading off a site for his furnace on Deer Creek, opposite the town, has sent below for fire-bricks and machinery, and is burning a kiln of charcoal for fuel. His idea is to raise a sufficient heat in the furnace to melt the rocks, run it off at a spout, contending that the gold, being so much heavier, will sink to the bottom and can then be taken out pure and solid. It is all right in theory, but I have not much faith in its success. To hear the investors talk, however, you would think they were already millionaires.

(NOTE.—It did not work. He could not separate the gold from the slag and the forty thousand dollars was a clear loss.)

CHAPTER XVII.

A FORMIDABLE INDICTMENT OF THE TURKEY THIEVES—AN OLD-TIME LEGAL DOCUMENT —HALED INTO COURT—THE TRIAL; THE VERDICT AND THE PENALTY—A SAFETY VALVE FOR THE WILD SPIRITS—THE JACKASS NOT FOR SALE—PARD'S TENDER HEART—HIS CONSIDERATION FOR BIRD AND BEAST AND AFFECTION FOR HIS CABIN MATE—THE DONKEY'S CORRECT PRINCIPLES.

149

A FORTY-NINER

CHAPTER XVII.

FEBRUARY 17, 1852.—The boys over on Selby Flat are having a bushel of fun in these slack times. When the inquest was held on Jack Ristine, it leaked out that there had been a turkey supper at his cabin. Two or three of the witnesses, who were on oath, gave it away under pressure, and the landlord, who has not yet got over being mad, applied to the justice of the peace for warrants for as many of those as he learned were at the feast. As he could not swear as to who stole the birds, he wanted them arrested as accessories to the crime. The judge refused to issue the warrants and the miners got hot and leagued together to quit patronizing both the hotel and bar-room. This brought him to his senses, he apologized and agreed to drop the matter. It gave the boys a hunch, especially those who had lost their bets, and for deviltry they called a miners' court, preferred charges against the lucky ones who had won their money, on the theory that they must have had guilty knowledge of the larceny or else they would not have been so anxious to bet. The charges were drawn up in mock legal form and were as full of "whereases," "whereins," "aforesaids," and "be it knowns" as a lawyer's brief. As I recall the document, it runs about as follows:

"Whereas, Before, on, about or preceding Christmas Day, some party or parties unknown to the complainants, but by strong and corroborative circumstantial evidence, suspected

to be (here followed about twenty names, including my own and my Saleratus Ranch friends), and

"Whereas, We believe these aforesaid named parties did feloniously, surreptitiously, not having the peace and dignity of Selby Flat, its hitherto untarnished and unstained name and reputation at heart, enter, break into and force open a certain coop known to have contained one dozen gobblers, and did abstract, take away, carry off and levant with the said birds, the aforesaid turkeys, being the property of the proprietor of the Selby Flat Hotel, and

"Whereas, Said gobblers having been provided, bought and procured for the delectation, comfort, sustenance and happiness of your petitioners, it being understood, agreed and promulgated that the aforesaid and before-named birds were to be roasted, stuffed, cooked, garnished and served to the denizens of Selby Flat, a town situated and being in and about Brush Creek, Nevada County, State of California, U. S. A., irrespective of previous condition, sex or color, at the rate of two dollars and fifty cents per capita, with mince pie and fixings thrown in, and

"Whereas, Said felonious abstraction wrought upon your petitioners great mental and physical anguish, disturbing their peace of mind as well as the dignity of Selby Flat, and

"Whereas, The above-named and aforesaid parties did, contrary to the Statutes of the Commonwealth (See Randall on non sequitur, vol. IV, page 32), enter into a conspiracy, based, founded upon and made possible by their guilty knowledge of the intended forcible and felonious abstraction of the previously mentioned gobblers, wheedle, entreat and coax innocent bystanders, to wit, your petitioners, to wager, hazard, and bet certain sums of money in regard to the presence of the aforesaid turkeys at a Christmas dinner, and

A FORTY-NINER

"Whereas, It is a well known and deep founded principle of common law, as well as an obiter dicta, in all well regulated sporting circles, that no man can take advantage of or profit by betting on a dead sure thing;

"Therefore, your petitioners respectfully pray this court, taking into consideration the heinousness and enormity of the offense, to adjudge the aforesaid and before-named parties of the first part guilty of foul murder, and that if the court and jury be inclined to mercy and should hesitate to impose capital punishment, that the least penalty to be meted out to these outlaws and disturbers of their neighbors' turkey roosts be the return to your innocent and defrauded petitioners of the monies they were induced to put up, chance, and risk on a game where the cards were stacked 'agin 'em'."

There was a lot more to it which I can't remember, and it was a gay afternoon consumed in taking testimony, swearing witnesses and making mock speeches. It was nearly dark before the trial was finished and the case submitted to the jury, which brought in a verdict without quitting their seats, of "Rape in the first degree." The sentence was drinks ad libitum for the town, and the landlord got even as the crowd patronized his bar with a free hand and purse.

After I went home and got to thinking it over it all seemed childish and foolish, but Pard differed with me. He argued that the lives we led were dismal enough and that anything that would break the monotony and furnish amusement was a safety valve. I guess he is right, for, nonsensical at it was, I enjoyed it as much as any of them. After all, there was a damper to it, for even at our wildest we could not help thinking of the mysterious fate of Ristine and Carter, and that the last we ever saw of them was when we were eating supper in their cabin.

FEBRUARY 24, 1852.—It has been fairly pleasant all the week, but we have done very little, as the water is still up in the creek and the drift is played out. Pard thinks he will make a trip to the Bay, and wants me to go along, but I don't feel like it just yet. We are both tired of loafing, and I think we would pull up and leave if we had not set our minds on working Rock Creek. We have our interests in our river claims, but we can't get into them before next August, at the earliest, and as our partners are willing to buy our shares, I think we will sell out to them. We have a fourth interest, and have been offered six thousand dollars for it by outsiders.

I have not answered Hetty's letter yet. It is a puzzle what to say to her. If she had not broken the engagement I should feel bound to stick, even if my feelings have changed, but she cannot expect to play fast and loose with me. To be honest, I love Marie more than any other woman on earth, and if she comes back and is in the same mind as when she went away, the chances are that we will make the match. The only hesitation I have is as to what the old folks will say, but I will take her back to them, and Marie is sure to win them over.

Pard is always growling about the jackass disturbing his rest and making him look foolish by trotting around after him like a dog, so I proposed, as we had no particular use for him, that we sell him. Gracious! he flared up and wanted to know if he did not have a right to associate with a jackass of his own choice, when I was running with a dozen or more. This was a fling at the crowd over at Selby Flat. I have been going over there two or three nights in a week not thinking that I was leaving Pard alone or that he cared much for my company. If it had not been for the twinkle in his eye I would have snapped back, but I saw he was not in earnest, so I replied if the beast and I were not enough jackasses for him he was welcome to get more. He said that he would acknowledge

that the jack didn't have a very tuneful voice and his song was not as melodious as that of some of the birds but he preferred his note to that of the blue jay, and insisted that he was an animal of good principles. He did not associate with bad company, drink whiskey or break any of the commandments, and if he, the donkey, was jackass enough to put trust in a man he was not going to abuse it. "The fact is, Alf," he said, "'Jack' (that's the dog) and he are great comforts to me. I have told them in confidence all about my past life and it doesn't seem to have lowered me in their opinion a bit. Under the circumstances I can't go back on either of them."

Pard is a queer stick. When I think it over I have never known him to kill animal, bird, or reptile, with the exception of the rattlesnake that struck at me on the trail, nor have I ever heard him say an unkind word of a living soul. He has been a big brother to me, and I can look back and see how happy we have been together, but still he insists that the obligation is on his side. The only thing in the future that troubles me is the possibility that our partnership will break up when we leave here.

CHAPTER XVIII.

JACKSON VISITS THE NEIGHBORING MINING
CAMPS—POCKET HUNTING AT ROUGH AND
READY—A PUZZLE FOR THE THEORISTS—
A SECTION OF A DEAD RIVER—SPECULATION
ON THE GENESIS OF GOLD——THE OLD-
TIMERS' DICTUM—FIRST VISIT TO THE THEA-
TER—PARD RETURNS FROM SAN FRANCISCO
—A PROFITABLE INVESTMENT—JACKSON DE-
CIDES TO MARRY HIS FRENCH SWEETHEART.

A FORTY-NINER

CHAPTER XVIII.

MARCH 2, 1852.—Pard left for San Francisco Monday, and I have been wandering over the country all the week. I rode over to Rough and Ready Tuesday and found a lively camp. The diggings have been very rich all around it and they have found on the ridge, near Randolph Flat, claims that have paid big. A peculiarity is the number of rich pockets that have been struck. A miner named Axtell uncovered one two weeks ago, from which he has taken out fourteen thousand dollars, and there have been any number that yielded from five hundred to five thousand dollars. There are miners who follow pocket mining exclusively, and there certainly is a fascination to it. They will work for weeks without making grub and then come across a pocket from which they will take out hundreds or thousands. As one of them said to me: "It's like playing a number on 'Red and Black.' You may make a hundred bets without winning a cent, but when it does come up you get a hundred for one." I guess we all like to gamble. There is a place below Nevada City that is like Rough and Ready in the way of deposits, and that is Red Hill. I am told that they find the gold there in little narrow clay streaks and when they discover one it is sure to be rich. It's a peculiar sort of gold, not nuggets or ordinary dust, but flaky and in thin leaves, and so light that a yeast powder can full will not weigh more than four or five ounces. It has been a puzzle to the mining sharps, as it knocks out all theories of gold coming down from the high mountains or out of the quartz veins exclusively. No one can, after seeing these flakes of gold,

159

sometimes two inches square and as thin as a wafer, stuck in the clay, dispute that it grew there. And here is another puzzle. I was over to Red Dog Wednesday and stayed there all night. The miners told me that for a couple of years mining there was about the same as around Nevada. Greenhorn Creek and the gulches and ravines were rich, but were all worked out. Last fall they ran into blue gravel cemented, which had paid well, and they are working along this streak for three miles or more. The queer thing is that the majority believe that their claims are in the bed of an old river, and to prove it they say that the bed-rock rises on both sides of a well defined channel, that all of the rocks and boulders are smooth and water-worn, and that they find petrified logs and impressions of leaves that floated down the stream when it was running.

This may all be, but how did it come that there are two hundred feet of clay (lava) on top, and how is it that a river could run up on the side of a mountain?

At the hotel that night there was a lot of discussion and argument as to how the gold came there, but none of them was very convincing. And old fellow said to me: "Never mind these scientific cusses. I'll give you the right one. Gold is just where you find it and you are as likely to come across it in one place as another." The next day I crossed over the trail to Grass Valley and had a look at the quartz mines. There is something that upsets all of our notions. In two or three places they have followed these veins of white, glassy rock down into the bed-rock for seventy-five feet and they don't seem to pinch out. I did not find anybody to explain how gold

(NOTE.—Jackson touches on a subject that in pioneer days furnished matter for elaborate discussion. The geologist and expert had not invaded the field at that time and in the early "Fifties" there were many theories, absurd and otherwise, as to the genesis of the gold deposits. The one generally accepted was that which attributed its origin to a huge vein or deposit high up in the mountains and this ignis fatuus lured many to long, weary and fruitless searches.)

A FORTY-NINER

got inside this hard rock, and I guess nobody knows. I saw on my way home that in the valley where we had the bear and jackass fight, the timber had been cut off, a race track laid out, and on Sunday night there is to be a quarter of a mile dash for two thousand dollars, between "Wake Up Jack"—a horse that belongs to the Nevada postmaster—and "Come Along Johnny"—a Marysville horse. I have never seen a race horse and believe that I will ride over to it. I'm getting to be real sporty. They have built a theater in Nevada, down over Deer Creek, and a company from Sacramento has been playing there all the week. I had never been to a play, so Friday night I went over and took it in. They played a piece called "The Stranger," and at first I could not see where the enjoyment came in. It was so ridiculous to see a lot of people upon a raised platform making believe something was happening that was real, when anybody in his right senses knew better, but before I realized it I was that interested in Mrs. Waller's troubles (what old-time theater-goer does not recall the weepy Mrs. Waller?) that I forgot where I was, that these were only play actors, and the tears rolled down my cheeks over the heroine's trials and sufferings. It came out all right and I must admit that the performance was worth the money.

Had a letter from Marie, which makes me feel a lot better. She says that she will surely come back in a month or two and that I must remember that the only reason for her return is to see me, as what little money she has invested in San Francisco would not be sufficient inducement for her to make a long, tiresome voyage. The letter was written the latter part of January, and it may be possible that she is now on her way. I have fully made up my mind that if she wants me she can have me, no matter what anybody thinks about it.

MARCH 9, 1852.—Pard got back from the Bay Monday night and came straight over to the cabin. We have done

nothing during the week but talk over our own affairs and plan for the future. He says San Francisco, in his opinion, is bound to be a large city, and that, even if the gold is all dug out of the country, it has resources enough to get along without it. We can clean up a profit of twenty-four thousand dollars on our land investments, but he is not going to sell out at that figure. If I don't want to stay he will give me fourteen thousand dollars for what I have put in, which includes principal and profits. That makes me worth over twenty thousand dollars, but I am not going to accept his offer for a while yet. We are both tired of the hard work and the hard fare of a miner's life. It was different when we were taking out of our claim forty or fifty ounces a week; but it is worked out, and, outside of our interest in the river claims and our project to wash over Rock Creek, there is nothing ahead. Pard says that his wife has agreed to join him in the spring, and would come at once if he would say the word. He has made up his mind, however, to brush up a little on the law (he brought a lot of law books back with him) and the old cabin is just the place to do his reading. Then in the spring he will go to San Francisco, provide a home for his wife and open an office. There is plenty of litigation, principally over the Spanish land grants and titles, and he is confident that he can work up a good practice. He has enough to live on now without touching his wife's money, so that that trouble cannot come between them again. Now he can see that he was unreasonable, and the greater part of the fault was on his side in asking her to live a poor man's life when she had plenty of money of her own, and was not brought up that way. He wants me to go along, and says that I can study law with him, but frankly tells me that he doesn't believe I will ever make a good lawyer, not that I have not got brains enough, but he doesn't think I have a legal mind or inclination. That is true. I never had any hankering to be a lawyer, doctor, or preacher.

A FORTY-NINER

On my side, I made a clean breast of it and confessed that there was an understanding between Madame Ferrand and myself, and when she came back from France we would visit the old folks together and then get married, but that neither she nor I had any idea of settling down in my old home. Pard said that it was that sort of a situation that any advice from him would be impertinent. He was most favorably impressed with the madame, if she returned it was proof of a sincere attachment, and that she was capable of a great, unreasoning love. It was not my money that she was after, for she had more than I. Beside, she was taking as many chances as I was. I showed him Hetty's last letter, and he said it was up to me to decide, although he knew without me telling him what the decision would be. If I had not come to California and had lived my life out on the farm, Hetty would have been the right sort of a helpmeet, but I had got out of the leading strings and would never be contented to fall back into that old rut. Not that I was not unsophisticated and anything but worldly wise, still I had grown too big for the Litchfield hills. Then he got sarcastic and remarked that, anyway, the woman I married would boss me, and that the madame would probably make the yoke easier than the little Puritan. All he asked was that after I had seen a little of the world I would come back to San Francisco, where we could be together, and he would keep us both straight. Dear old boy! He does not like the idea of our parting, and neither do I. Well, our talk settled it. We will stay here until spring, not bothering to work very much, and then leave to carry out our plans.

I went over to the race at Hughes' track this afternoon. There was a big crowd and a lot of excitement and reckless betting. There were a half dozen Marysville sports on hand and they backed their horse without stint. "Wake Up Jack," the Nevada horse, won the race by ten feet in a distance of a

quarter of a mile, and they say the home gamblers were ahead more than twenty thousand dollars. Just for fun, I ventured a hundred dollars on "Wake Up Jack," and gained that much. I have said nothing to Pard about it, as he would surely give me a lecture on the folly of it. I note one thing, whenever I am around where gambling is going on I have an inclination to join in and I can now understand why so many miners are inveterate gamblers. The best way is to keep away from it and out of temptation.

The remains of Carter's body were found last week near the head of Myers Ravine, about a mile from his cabin. There was nothing but the skull bones, gnawed clean, and his shirt, overalls and boots; but the hair was the same color, and in the pocket of the overalls there were a knife, pipe and tobacco pouch that were known to have belonged to him. No sort of theory as to their deaths fits the case. It was not robbery. If it had been a quarrel and they had killed each other, their bodies would not have been found a mile apart. So far as known, they lived on the best of terms, and they were good fellows who had no enemies. It is not likely that both went crazy and wandered off to die. Some think that they may have accidentally poisoned themselves; but it is all guess-work and a great mystery.

(NOTE.—It may be added that it was a mystery that was never solved, and in those stirring times, when incident followed incident so rapidly, the memory of it soon faded from men's minds.)

CHAPTER XIX.

PARD BRUSHES UP IN HIS PROFESSION—NO DEFERENCE PAID TO WEALTH—HOW FORTUNE FAVORED JENKINS—WHEN YOU HAVE GOT THE LUCK, IT'S WITH YOU FROM START TO FINISH—JIM VINEYARD'S HARD STREAK—A MOVING TALE OF A MISSED OPPORTUNITY—ONE MAN'S LOSS ANOTHER MAN'S GAIN—TROUSERS POCKETS VS. MONEY BELTS.

CHAPTER XIX.

MARCH 16, 1852.—When we thought the rain over and a few weeks of good weather due, it began to storm again, and it is now worse than ever. My companion does not mind it, as he has settled down to studying his law books, and the rain is an excuse not to buckle to hard work again. In fact, if we carry out our project to work Rock Creek, he proposes to hire a substitute, as he pretends to be rusty in his profession and needs all the time he will have to spare to brush up before we go to San Francisco. I have no profession to study up and the hours hang heavy on my hands. I have written the old folks that I will be home early in the summer, and they are delighted. So am I, with the exception that I am not certain exactly how they are going to take to Marie. A foreigner and a Papist— what a shock that will be to mother, saying nothing about the gossip of my boyhood friends and neighbors. I will trust Marie to win her way with the old folks, and don't care a snap of my finger about the rest of them. On the other hand, what a big man I will be back there, returned from California with a sack full of gold, and the richest man in the village, with the exception of old Squire Battell! What little difference it makes to us here whether a man has money or not. I know half a dozen men on Selby Hill who have taken out in the past year anywhere from forty thousand to sixty thousand apiece, and a dozen more who have made still more than that from mining ground on Gold Flat, Coyoteville and Manzanita Hill. They don't put on any airs and nobody envies them. We

don't ask what a man is worth or how much he has got. The
only question is, is he a good fellow? If he is, he is one of
us; if he isn't, we let him alone. Even brains and education
do not count for very much and some of the most ignorant
are the most prosperous. Mining is not a complicated process, and, as far as I can see, is more a question of luck than
anything else. A miner from Auburn was telling me the
other day of a case that happened there last summer. A man
named Jenkins was working at the head of Missouri Gulch,
"tomming." His diggings were just fair, about half an ounce
a day. He had built a little dirt reservoir to catch what water
there was, which was very scarce. The gulch headed in a flat
and up at the end of it, where it rose up to the hills, there was
a running spring, the water seeping into the flat and going to
waste. In order to make his own supply hold out, he dug a
narrow trench and ran the seepage into his reservoir. It
worked all right for a few days and he paid no further attention to it, not even going up on the flat for a week. One morning he noticed that the water was not running in the ditch
and, supposing that a gopher had tapped it, he put his shovel
on his shoulder and walked along the trench to see what the
trouble might be. When about half way across he was aston-
ished to see that the bottom of his ditch for twenty feet or
more was one yellow mass of gold. It was an immense rotten quartz deposit, and inside of a month he had taken out
forty-one thousand dollars. That was surely blind luck; still,
there was another phase of it that was luckier. The flat was
unclaimed ground, open to location by anybody. The gold
must have been there in plain view day and night for a week
or more. Miners were tramping around in every direction
hunting diggings, yet by pure chance not one happened to
cross the flat that week. Fortune started in to favor Jenkins
and did not make any half work of it. As my friend said,
"It just shows that when you've got the luck, it's with you

from start to finish." Then he rounded off with what he called a hard luck story. The mountains are full of miners tramping around from one section to another, wandering over the country, men leaving with their piles or hunting better diggings, and there are numerous hold-ups and murders on the trails that become known only when somebody runs across the bodies. As we are all strangers to each other outside of our immediate neighborhoods, the identity of the murdered man is rarely discovered and but little interest is taken in apprehending the murderers. Jim Vineyard, who was mining a bar on the Middle Fork of the Yuba (Vineyard was father-in-law of Cherley De Long of Marysville, afterward Congressman from Nevada and U. S. Minister to Japan) was up to the store on Kanaka Creek one Sunday, having a good time with a crowd of the boys, and remarked that he had struck a streak of mighty hard luck during the week. "What's the matter, Jim, isn't the claim paying?" asked one of his friends. "Oh, h——l, the claim is all right; it was this way, you see. I was working on the mine Thursday afternoon, windlassing gravel, when I saw a floater (a drowned man) come bobbing down the river and it drifted on to the upper edge of the bar. It was some poor miner who had fallen in somewhere up the stream. I went through his pockets to see if there was anything that would reveal who he was; but found nothing except a knife, plug of tobacco and a buckskin purse with three hundred dollars of dust in it. Of course, I kept the purse, as somebody might recognize it and prove his identity." Jim paused to take another drink and the crowd did not seem to catch the point.

"I don't see anything very unlucky about that," interjected his friend. "You don't," retorted Jim. "Wait until you hear the rest of it. I was too busy and too tired to haul the body out and bury it, so I just gave it a shove and let it float along down stream. Jack Batterson is fluming about

a mile below my bar and the fool corpse had to jam into the head of his flume, instead of going on down the river to the plains. If it had, then I would never have known how mean fortune could be. Just why Jack stripped its clothes off, I don't know; any sensible, sympathetic man that had the interest of the corpse at heart would have dug a hole and put it under ground, clothes and all, but he didn't; maybe he wanted the clothes for an extra suit; anyway, he took them off and I'm d——d if he didn't find a money belt around the waist with twelve hundred dollars more in dust inside, and now he is crowing over me because I was not smart enough to make a better search. If you don't call that hard luck, then I don't know what the article is."

The crowd agreed that it was pretty tough on Jim and proceeded to help him forget it by ordering drinks all around.

I must say I was a little shocked by the heartlessness of the incident, although my friend contended that it was a good joke on Jim, and it was so regarded by everybody on the Middle Fork.

CHAPTER XX.

THE UNSOCIABLE COUPLE ON ROUND MOUN-
TAIN—GOOD FELLOWSHIP AMONG THE PIO-
NEERS—THE TAX-COLLECTOR PASSES THE
MINERS BY—A WOMAN IN BREECHES—MARIE
RETURNS FROM FRANCE—ADOPTION OF A
NEW METHOD OF SLUICING—THE DOG AND
DONKEY STRIKE UP A FRIENDSHIP—FRANK
DUNN AND HIS ECCENTRICITIES—POSING AS
A HORRIBLE EXAMPLE.

A FORTY-NINER

CHAPTER XX.

MARCH 23, 1852.—There is a queer couple living up on the slope of Round Mountain at the gap where it breaks off into the Rock Creek Canon. All sorts of stories and rumors about them and their doings have been in circulation, although nobody had any acquaintance with them or knew any facts about their operations. It was noticed, however, that they never were away from the cabin at the same time, that they made no friends or visits and that when anyone came around their neighborhood they were gruff and unsocial. As this is a great country for everybody minding his own business, no attention would have been paid to them if their manners and customs had not been so different from the general rule. If there is one thing above another that prevails, it is the goodfellowship among us all. If a man is taken sick, is hurt, or in bad luck, there is not one of us that is not ready to nurse him or put our hands into our pockets if necessary. We don't ask who he is, where he came from or what is his religion. On the other hand, men are coming and going all the time. You may have known a man for a year, then you miss him, see a stranger at his cabin, and ask what has become of the old occupant and the answer will be, "Oh, he has made his pile and gone back to the States," or, "His claim petered out and he's off prospecting," or, "He went with the rush to Gold Bluff, or the Kern River excitement," and then you forget him. It's all a hurly-burly with nobody making plans to live here permanently. We were talking about this over at

Selby Flat the other night and the crowd was unanimous in denouncing the extravagance of a project that was being agitated to build a brick courthouse at Nevada City. No matter how much gold is discovered, it cannot last always—not more than a few years at most—and when it is gone what will there be to keep up a town, or to live for, and then all of the money spent on stone buildings and courthouses will go to waste.

I don't suppose I ought to growl about it. So far as I know, the tax-collector does not bother us miners. Our log cabins are not worth taxing, our claims are exempt, and if the town people want to pay for these follies, it is their privilege. The outside towns—Grass Valley, Rough and Ready and Selby Flat—are doing some lively kicking over the courthouse scheme, and there is talk of a fight to take away the county seat from Nevada City.

Out of curiosity I rode over to see the couple who live on Round Mountain, and I made a funny discovery. If one of them is not a woman dressed in men's clothes, then I don't know a woman when I see one. The cabin is a queer sort of shanty, about thirty feet long, built into the bank so that the roof comes down even with it. There are two doors, one narrow and the other five feet wide. There is a wheelbarow track leading out of the wide door to a dump-pile of waste dirt and a Tom set in the ravine below, where, evidently, the pay dirt is washed. I could see at once that they were tunneling into the hill from the back of the cabin, although if it had not been for the dump-pile, Long Tom and wheelbarrow track no one would have suspected that any mining was going on in the vicinity. While I was sitting on my horse taking in all this, a slight young fellow came out wheeling a barrow of dirt. He seemed startled to see me, turned his head away, dumped his dirt, pulled his hat down over his eyes and went back through the door without even saying

good morning. I started to ride away when another man appeared at the door—a long-whiskered, stout-built fellow who did not seem to be at all pleased at my being there—and asked me roughly what I wanted. I replied that I wanted nothing, was riding around the country, happened to come across the place, had halted a minute and that was all. He turned to go back, hesitated, then looked around and asked me to get down and hitch the horse. I was so curious that I accepted the invitation and in a few minutes we were sitting out on the dump-pile in the sun chatting away like old friends. I think he is a Western man by his accent, not that I asked any questions, not having the chance. He did the questioning, and kept me busy answering, not seeming to know anything about what was going on anywhere, neither in his own neighborhood nor abroad, and although he did not appear to be an ignorant man in a general way, he certainly lacked information on current happenings. The young fellow failed to show up, and, after an hour or so, the man excused himself for a minute—it was past noon—came back and asked me if I would not stop for dinner. I was dying to see the inside of the cabin and accepted. Well, you never saw a neater place. Twenty feet of it was partitioned off. There was a board floor, swept and clean, a curtain to the window, paper, the edges cut in scallops, on the shelves, a home-made double bed nicely made up, and pillows. The table was covered with a table-cloth made of flour sacks sewn together, but white and clean, and the crockery all washed since breakfast. I wondered what sort of finicky miners these could be, so different in their housekeeping from the rest of us, when the young fellow began to put the grub on the table. That settled it. He had his hat off, and "he" was a woman dead sure. If there had been nothing else, the cooking would have proved it: hot biscuit, fried quail with a thin strip of bacon wrapped around them, beans, of course, but not greasy beans, a fine

cup of coffee, and doughnuts. Gracious! That was the first doughnut I had eaten since leaving Connecticut. He just introduced her as his partner without any explanation and I did not ask for any, although it looked funny to see a pretty, black-haired, black-eyed woman dressed up in a woolen shirt, overalls and boots. I had sense enough to keep my mouth shut on the subject and we ate our dinner as if there was nothing strange in the situation. After it was over and we had smoked our pipes, she in the meantime clearing off the table and washing the dishes, he asked me to come in and look at his mine. He had run a tunnel into the mountain from the back of his cabin and was in a hundred feet or more. He said he had stumbled on it by accident, built the cabin as I saw it, just for a notion, that it had paid and was still paying very well and he would stay with it until it was worked out. He came out with me when I got ready to go away, shook hands and asked me to ride over again, and then said that he knew that he had the reputation of being unsociable and eccentric; that maybe he was, but if I got acquainted I would find out he was not a bad sort; that while it seemed as if there was a mystery there really wasn't, and there was not much to tell. If I made him another visit he would explain, not because he had to, but that he could understand how it looked queer to an outsider. Then he got sort of gruff and said it was nobody's business but his own, and I rode away. Pard and I talked it over and we agreed that the woman was without doubt his wife, who preferred to live with her husband in this way rather than be separated. If they wanted to lead hermit lives they had the right. Really, the only strange part of it is her dressing in men's clothes and working in the mine. I would not let any wife of mine do that sort of thing.

MARCH 30, 1852.—After all my doubts and fears Marie arrived in San Francisco by the last steamer, and I got a letter

from her yesterday. She says she will spend a week or ten days there and will then come to Nevada, and that I am not to come to meet her, but wait until she arrives. Pard says I am too absurdly happy to be in my right mind, and I guess I am, although a week is a long time to wait and I have had a notion to go down after her anyway. Instead, however, we began setting our sluices in the bed of the creek, the water having run down so as not to interfere very much, and Pard is as tired of reading as I am of loafing. It has taken us all of the week to get the boxes in place and we will begin sluicing in the dirt to-morrow. We are going to try the same plan on the creek that we did on the flat, ground-sluice the dirt and let it run through the sluices. We found out that on Deer Creek they have adopted another plan, doing away with cross riffles and forking out, and, instead, paving some of the boxes with cobbles and the rest with heavy slats and Hungarian riffles. If this works all right we can put a lot of dirt through, as there is plenty of water and fall for a tailrace.

The country is looking fine. Since the rain quit and the sun shone, the grass is up three inches on the hillsides and the oaks and sycamores are leaving out. The horses and jackass are rolling fat, and even Jack seems to like the coming of spring time. He has got to be a very sedate and serious dog. He and the jackass have struck up a great friendship and wander over the hills together all day long, but invariably bring up at the cabin when night comes on. We stake out the horses, as they might feed off too far and be stolen, or lost, if we let them run loose. Mother writes me that she surely expects me home in June and that I must not break my word. I don't think I will go back on it. It will all be decided as soon as I see Marie.

Another miner lost his life through whiskey. Bill Grace, who had been having a night of it over in Nevada, started for home about midnight on Tuesday. He disappeared, and

his partner, who could get no trace of him in town, or elsewhere, found his body Thursday in an old shaft on Selby Hill. There was about ten feet of water in the shaft and, of course, he was drowned. There is a good deal of complaint about these old abandoned shafts and there is talk of the miners taking some action to compel the claim owners to cover them up. It is dangerous even for sober men to walk around dark nights.

Frank Dunn, of Nevada, was over to see Pard yesterday. He is one of the brightest lawyers in the State, and liked by everybody, but he has a bad failing. He will go on long sprees and is so uncertain in his habits that his clients lose faith in him. He made a proposition to Pard to form a partnership and practice together, but Pard declined; he is set in his determination to go to San Francisco.

They tell many amusing stories of Dunn and his habits. They found him one day setting in the street in the sun, his back against the liberty pole on the Plaza, owlishly viewing the surroundings. One of his friends remonstrated and tried to persuade him to seek the obscurity of his room. "What for?" said Dunn. "Is there anything in the statutes of the State of California contrary to my occupying the small space which I have preempted on this highway? Is there any reason, if I am so minded, that I should not teach my fellow citizens the great moral lesson of the overthrow and debasement of genius by the Demon Rum? Am I not better employed than if in a stifling, tobacco perfumed courtroom, beating law into the skull of a thick-headed judge, who don't know Black-

(NOTE.—Dunn was all that Jackson says, a bright lawyer and a leader of the early Nevada bar. In the old days his witty sayings, idiosyncrasies and queer bibulous fancies were talked of and repeated by everybody in the county. He died, I believe, in 1856, and is buried in the old Pine Tree Graveyard.)

stone from white quartz? No, I will not remove myself from the public gaze unless,"—here he hesitated and winked his eye at his friend—"unless you should happen to have four bits about you and should ask me to join you. That would be a moving and persuasive argument not to be resisted. Ah! you have, help me up"—and he was persuaded.

CHAPTER XXI.

A SUCCESSFUL EXPERIMENT—A JOKE ON THE
VISITORS—ROAD AGENTS HOLD UP A STAGE
—UNCHIVALRIC TREATMENT OF THE WOM-
AN PASSENGER—MEETING OF THE LOVERS—
JACKSON'S WORD PICTURE OF THE BEAU-
TIES OF THE LANDSCAPE, VIEWED FROM
SUGAR LOAF—THE RECONCILIATION OF AN-
DERSON AND WIFE—MARIE'S COMMENTS.

A FORTY-NINER

CHAPTER XXI.

APRIL 3, 1852.—We buckled down to sluicing in the creek Monday morning, and as we had plenty of water we put through a pile of dirt. It was working in the dark, for neither one of us knew whether we were saving any gold or not. I had my doubts and Pard was not sure, as the stuff ran through with a rush and it did not seem as if the riffles would catch the gold. It began to rain Friday night and we cleaned up the best we could Saturday morning, as we knew the creek would rise and carry out our sluices unless we got them up on the bank. We were agreeably surprised to find that we had caught fourteen ounces. Most of it was very fine, but there was a little coarse gold the size of pumpkin seeds and one nugget that weighed nine dollars. While not wonderfully rich it will pay pretty good wages. It will take three or four days to get our boxes set back in the creek, and, as it is liable to rain more or less during April, we have concluded not to try it again until the first of the month. By that time the winter rains will be over.

We had a good joke on John Hall and Delos Calkins this morning. I have got so I can speak French fairly well, and when the boys dropped over on a visit Pard and I jabbered away at each other in that language, throwing in a little English to Delos and John occasionally when they broke into the conversation. They listened awhile, but got more and more disgusted, and finally Delos said: "You think you are smart, but I think you are a couple of d——n fools. What is it,

Choctaw or Greek?" We told him it was French and that it was our custom to converse with each other in that polite language, and he said we were a pair of galoots, who didn't know the difference between French and Patagonian. He offered to bet us an ounce apiece that we could not tackle the proprietor of the Hotel de Paris in Nevada and throw that lingo at him for five minutes without being taken for lunatics and chucked out into the street. Then he began to grin as if he had caught on to a new idea and said: "Why, of course, he's going to talk to her in her own language, 'Parley vous Francais, Madam?'" How they got on to it I don't know, but the boys all know that Marie is coming back and that there is something in the wind; so part of the joke was on me after all.

We had a talk with them about our new method of mining on Rock Creek, and they have taken the pointer and are going to work a portion of Brush Creek the same way. We told them part of our plans and that we are going to leave the country early in the summer and they were genuinely sorry to hear it. They like me, but are specially fond of Anderson. He has been a sort of umpire in all of the disputes that have arisen and a peacemaker in the neighborhood of quarrels. They made up their minds to run him for the Legislature next election, but our going away spoils their plans. After they left Pard said that before he went away he intended to get them all together, give them a blow-out and then tell them his real name and why he had sailed under false colors. He felt that he had to do it, both in justice to them and himself.

The country above and all the trails have been infested with a gang of highwaymen for the past three months and it has not been safe to travel, as they robbed and murdered right and left. It is Reelfoot Williams' gang and he and his followers do not seem to be afraid of anything or anybody. Wednesday morning they held up the Nevada stage near

A FORTY-NINER

Illinoistown and they got away with seventy-five hundred dollars. There were only two passengers aboard, a man and a woman. He gave up two hundred and thirty dollars, all that he had. She swore she did not have any money, but they were mean enough to search her and, although she fought like a tiger cat, it did not do her any good. Sure enough, they found six slugs (fifty dollars each) in her stockings, which they confiscated, and rode away laughing. The man said that she came pretty near getting even in the tongue lashing she gave them, and that, until he heard her tirade, he did not know that the English language had such possibilities.

APRIL 13, 1852.—I went over to Nevada both Monday and Tuesday afternoons to meet the stage, thinking that possibly Marie might be aboard, but she wasn't. I swore I would not go again until I heard from her, but I guess I would if she had not saved me the trouble, for about three o'clock Wednesday afternoon Pard and I were sitting out under the tree, and I was thinking about saddling the horse and taking a ride, when Jack began to bark, and here she came riding down the trail as pretty a sight as ever I saw. My heart beat like a trip hammer, my head felt dizzy, and I did not have sense enough to help her off her horse. Pard saved me the trouble, for which I didn't thank him, but she paid no attention to him; she just flung her arms around my neck and began laughing and crying and calling me "monchere." I was mightily embarrassed for a minute, until I saw out of the tail of my eye Pard and Jack disappearing up the trail. Then I gave her as warm and loving a welcome as she had me. Wasn't it lucky that we weren't working, and I had on clean clothes? I hitched her horse and then we sat down on the clean pine needles holding each other's hands, and if I lived a thousand years I never could write down half we said in the next hour. Gracious! Isn't she pretty with her crinkly brown hair, her

laughing eyes and her white teeth. I never realized before how handsome she is. I sprung my French on her and she just laughed and said I spoke it so well that she could understand some of it. After a while Pard strolled back, patted her hand and told her that to see me happy was to make him the same; all that I wanted was a good wife, and he was sure that she would make me one; that he loved me as well as if I was his own brother and then he choked and whistled to Jack and started for the trail again, but we would not let him go. We discussed all of our plans and came to a mutual understanding. Pard got supper—I was too busy talking and had no appetite anyhow—and about ten o'clock we both rode to Nevada with her, for the sake of the proprieties, as Pard put it. That, to me, was the happiest evening of all my life. Since then she has been over every day, generally getting here about nine o'clock in the morning—she has a room at the Hotel de Paris—stays until after supper and then I ride back with her in the twilight. I don't think there is any other place on earth where the evenings are as beautiful as they are here. We ride up to Sugar Loaf gap and look off on the country, the sky all aglow with the setting sun, a great ball of red fire dropping down behind the Yuba ridge, Deer Creek winding down the canon, the pine trees on the opposite slope standing out like black giants against the background, and as the darkness falls the lights twinkle and flash in the town lying at our feet, a breeze stirring as soft and caressing as—well, I am at a loss for words, but it is just good to live. When I tell Pard of it he says: "Yes, you're in love and every prospect pleases." Poor old Pard, he watches us as if we were a couple of children. She has petted, played and fondled Jack until the old dog has about thrown off the rest of us. Pard says he used to have a dog and two jackasses, and now he has only a single jackass left. Marie has coaxed him into telling his story and she says: "You poor man, you tried to throw away the best

thing on earth, a good woman's love." He pleads guilty, but insists that he repented in time. It is settled that Pard's wife will meet him in San Francisco in June.

We had a marriage up at Scott's ranch last week and Marie and I went to it by invitation. Lou Hanchett, the boss miner on the ridge, has been courting a pretty girl at Selby Flat. They were friends of the Scotts, and the wedding was held at their place. About twenty of the boys from Selby Flat were there, as well as all of the miners from Rock Creek. Lou provided a big blow-out and ended up with a dance, which we kept up until midnight and then scattered. Hanchett is one of the best fellows in the country, but the boys are not exactly pleased with his capturing the belle of the county and taking her away from the Flat.

(NOTE.—Hanchett and wife settled at the camp afterward known as Moores Flat, where he discovered and opened one of the richest mines in the State. A girl baby was born to them in 1853, who passed her girlhood in that pretty mountain town. She married George Crocker, son of Charles Crocker, one of the original projectors and builders of the Central Pacific Railroad, and died in Paris two years ago. Lou Hanchett and wife still survive and are living in San Francisco at the present time.)

CHAPTER XXII.

A PLACID LIFE—MARIE OBSERVES THE PROPRIE-
TIES—PARD PLANS FOR THE FUTURE—THE
PROGRESS OF A LOVE IDYLL—REELFOOT
WILLIAMS AND HIS GANG—JACK'S WARNING
—ROBBERY OF THE BLUE TENT STORE—A
FRUITLESS PURSUIT—NEGOTIATING THE
SALE OF MINING PROPERTIES—SHALLOW
PLACERS WORKED OUT AND DEEP DIGGINGS
TAKE THEIR PLACE.

A FORTY-NINER

CHAPTER XXII.

APRIL 20, 1852.—It's a queer life we are leading, but it could not be pleasanter. I have given her my horse to ride and Pard lets me use his animal. Mine is the gentler one and I would not trust Marie on a bucking horse. Pard says that in the present state of affairs a jackass will do him. The landlady of the Hotel de Paris and Marie are countrywomen, and are great friends, which makes it very pleasant, as she has a companion to live with and it stops talk. Marie gets her breakfast at the hotel and then rides out to the cabin. Then we sit around in the shade until dinner time. Marie calls it *dejeuner a la fourchette*, and says dinner time doesn't come until six o'clock. We've hunted the town for dainty things to eat and have a regular picnic cooking our meals. It's astonishing to see how neat we have got to be, beds made up, dishes washed, cabin tidied up as clean as we can make it, and we have even swept the dooryard. Marie rubs her finger over the plates and shows us the grease on them and says : "We have not used of ze soap plenty enough" and "ze dish cloths, they are so dirty." Pard calls her a little tyrant, but he is as pleased as a boy, and Jack has gone daffy. Some of the afternoons when it is not too hot we ride together over the hills, but generally sit around under the pine trees chatting and planning the future. Pard is set on my going into some kind of business at San Francisco. First of all, though, we will visit the old folks, although not to settle down there. Marie says: "Perhaps ze fazzer and ze muzzer zey will not like it

t'at I take zere boy, but I t'ink I will make zem to love me,"
and Pard says she is a pretty witch whom nobody could help
liking. Then she wants me to visit Paris and meet her mother
and sisters and then, "if San Francisco," shrugging her shoulders, "well, what ze husband he desire, ze good wife she
should do ze same." Pard roars at this and says good doctrine before marriage, but wait until afterwards.

We rubbed pretty close to a nasty adventure Thursday.
Reelfoot Williams' gang has been raiding the trails and roads
for the past month. Posses have been raised to chase and cap-
ture them, and there was a fight two weeks ago between the
robbers and a Marysville posse down below Rose's Bar. A
deputy sheriff and one of his men were killed, but the thieves
got off scot free. We have heard of them around Nevada
County, and they held up the stage near Illinoistown a couple
of weeks ago. We had just about finished dinner when Jack
growled and Pard went to the door to find out what the trouble was. He saw a lot of men coming up the trail about fifty
yards away, and it popped into his mind that they were the
highwaymen. He jumped back and grabbed his rifle and I
followed suit with the shotgun and pistol. We both stood in
the door and when they rode up they saw we were heeled and
had the advantage of being inside. They halted, hesitated a
minute, the leader fell back and said something to one of the
men, and then asked if they were on the Blue Tent trail. Pard
answered, "Yes, keep right along and you will get there."

(NOTE.—It will be seen that Jackson's diary has degenerated or risen, as the
reader is pleased to view it, into a love romance, pure and simple, and the prosaic
facts of his existence do not get the same detail as before, but the situation is
idyllic. That this hard-headed Yankee and vivacious Frenchwoman should drift
together from opposite ends of the earth and form a mutual attachment that ignored
family ties, opposing religions and contrary views from almost any standpoint,
brave the sneers and criticisms of the world, each with an abiding faith in the other's
affection, constitutes a romantic episode, and, I was about to add, a strange one. I
qualify this, however, for I can recall dozens of instances that were quite as unreasonable from a commonplace standpoint. Love has no reasons, no excuses, and
the sexual instinct will not be denied.)

A FORTY-NINER

The spokesman, a good-looking fellow with long, light hair and mustache, wanted to know if we took them for a lot of d——n robbers, and Pard replied: "Never mind what we take you for, move along"; and they went. After they were out of sight Pard said I had better take Marie back to Nevada and he would go along and raise a posse. Marie was as courageous as either one of us and kept as quiet as a mouse while

(NOTE.—Reelfoot Williams, who is credited with being the leader of the gang of highwaymen mentioned in the diary, was a notorious desperado of the early days, and, so far as known, the first to organize a gang of murderers and thieves for systematic predatory work on the roads and trails. He first became locally known at Downieville, Sierra County, as a gambler and suspected robber, his chief source of income being derived from holding up miners on the trails and relieving them of their coin and gold dust. He was arrested in 1851 for highway robbery, and escaped conviction after a hard fought legal battle. In this connection, a story is told of his encounter, shortly after his trial, with the judge before whose court he had been arraigned. When Sierra County was organized in 1850, one Chap Schaffer secured the appointment, an all round good fellow, as good fellows were estimated in those days. He had a smattering of law, and occupied the bench to the satisfaction of the people, who did not demand too much learning or profundity. It was not held against him that he would at any time adjourn court to participate in a lively poker game, or that his salary and fees were dissipated at the faro banks. The day after the acquittal in Schaffer's court of Reelfoot Williams, the judge had business in one of the adjacent mining camps and, mounting his mule, started on his journey. When half way up the Slug Canon trail a man stepped out of the chaparral ordered him to throw up his hands and deliver his valuables.

The judge obeyed without hesitation so far as elevating his hands, but, recognizing the highwayman, exclaimed in perturbed tones: "Good Lord, Williams! I haven't got a cent, the boys cleaned me out in a little game last night."

Williams lowered his pistol with a "Hello, judge, is that you? I didn't know you or I wouldn't have held you up. I knew I had no chance against those Downieville sports. But say, judge, do me a favor, will you? Hurry on, there's another fellow coming up the trail and I've got to get out of this d—— country somehow."

The judge, much relieved in mind if not in pocket, stood not on the order of his going and, digging his spurs into the mule, started off at a lively gait. The other fellow was duly halted and Williams secured seven hundred dollars. It was after this exploit that he associated himself with Rattlesnake Dick and three others and started out as a full-fledged "road agent." The band held together until 1853, when three of its members were killed in an encounter with a sheriff's posse near Forbestown, Yuba County. Williams and Rattlesnake Dick escaped and fled to the southern country. Dick was stabbed and killed by a rival desperado at Spanish Dry Diggings in '54. Williams disappeared from view for several years, but turned up in the "sixties" in that paradise of roughs and bad men, Virginia City, Nev., where he flourished as "chief" to the annoyance of other aspirants to that coveted title, one of whom poked a shotgun through a saloon window and emptied a charge of buckshot into his carcass, bringing his career to an abrupt termination.)

193

they were at the cabin, but on the way to town tried to coax me not to go with the party, said that thief catching was not my business, and so did Pard, but I was not going to let him take any chances that I was not willing to share, even if he was a deputy sheriff. So I went. We might as well have stayed at home for all the good it did, although we found out we were right in thinking them highwaymen. An hour after they left us they robbed the Blue Tent store of a lot of provisions and eight hundred dollars in dust. It was five o'clock before we started and dark by the time we reached Blue Tent. We pushed on to Humbug (now North Bloomfield) but they had not been seen there and we figured out that they had gone down the ridge toward Cherokee. We went there the next day, but they had kept out of view and we heard no more of them. I got a good sight of the party at the cabin. There were five of them, three white men and two greasers. The fellow who did the talking was without doubt the leader, Williams, the other two were Rattlesnake Dick and Jim Mosely, and the two Mexicans, Alverez and Garcia. We have not the least doubt that they had intended to rob us, and would have done so if Jack had not given us warning. Good old Jack, he showed right there that he is worth all the trouble he ever gave us.

APRIL 27, 1852.—It has not rained for ten days and we will be able to get back into the creek again if we do not have any more showers. Neither Pard nor I are very anxious to continue mining and we have an offer from some of the Brush Creek boys which we may take up. We told them the result of our first week's washing and they proposed to come over and work with us a week, and if it yielded as well as in the beginning they would form a company to run it on shares and give us twenty per cent. of what they took out. We have agreed to their proposal and will begin putting in the boxes as soon

A FORTY-NINER

as the water runs down a little more. I am anxious to get away, but Pard says he will not leave until the time comes to meet his wife. She will start from New York the 21st of May. I asked Marie what we should do and she says that while there is nothing to keep her here except my convenience, still, after all Pard had done for me, and considering what our relations may be in the future, we had better postpone our complete happiness for a little while. Pard is much pleased over our decision.

We have bargained to sell our interests in the river claim to the other members of the company for six thousand dollars. If the creek turns out well, I will have pretty close to twenty-five thousand dollars, so I am comparatively a rich man. Marie tells me that she has twenty thousand dollars in French Rentes, which, as I understand it, are government bonds; the five thousand dollars invested in Frisco lots, and a country place near Paris, for which she paid fourteen thousand dollars. This place she wants her mother and sisters to live in, rent free, if I am willing, and they have enough income of their own to get along on nicely. As if I were going to have anything to say about what she does with her money! I will never touch a cent of it, although she insists that when we are married it is mine. Pard says she has it well invested and not to disturb it, as I have enough of my own to go into business or speculate with.

I notice that the miners now, instead of mining alone, or with a single partner, as was generally the rule at first, have got to forming companies of half a dozen or a dozen men and working their claims more systematically and extensively. Ounce diggings are not as easily found as they were a year or two ago and the creeks, gulches, and shallow placers are pretty well worked out. There are a lot of deep diggings, mostly operated by means of shafts, and some of these are down as much as one hundred and fifty feet.

On Coyote and Manzanita Hills they have rigged up whims, and hoist the dirt by horsepower, and at Red Dog and its vicinity they have built water wheels, which they use both to pump and raise the gravel. There is a lot of improvement in mining methods since we first began and I suppose there will be a lot more before the gold is all taken out of the ground.

CHAPTER XXIII.

A COMBINATION TO WORK ROCK CREEK—EX-
TRACTING GOLD FROM BLUE CEMENT—THE
CRITICAL CATS AT SELBY FLAT—FRENCH
COOKING IN THE OLD CABIN—THE INFLUX
OF CHINAMEN INTO THE MINES—A JOINT
VISIT TO ROUND MOUNTAIN—MARIE PRE-
DICTS AN EXPLOSION—NO CAUSE FOR INTER-
FERENCE.

A FORTY-NINER

CHAPTER XXIII.

MAY 4, 1852.—We got our sluice boxes back in the creek, finishing yesterday, and John Dunn and three of his partners will start in to-morrow morning. They are going to adopt the same plan that we tried, using as big a head of water as the boxes will carry, and ground-sluice all of the gravel through with as little handling as possible. The bed-rock will have to be creviced and cleaned by hand. If it pays they will make the same proposition to Platt and Dixon. They have enough ground of ours to keep them busy all summer. Dunn and his crowd are taking up all of the vacant ground on Brush Creek and will work it in the same way. It is a pity we did not know enough two years ago to wash the ground through sluices, instead of rocking it. We could have cleaned up a fortune in a month. We thought when the Long Tom came in, that it would never be improved upon. Now one rarely sees either rocker or Tom except in dry gulches and ravines where water is scarce.

I was over on Gopher Point a short time ago. The miners are having lots of trouble getting gold out of the cement. They run some of it through sluices, but the water has but little effect on it, and half of it goes into the tailrace without

(NOTE.—Jackson was speculating on the availability of gravel deposits that a few years afterward, when hydraulicing came into vogue, proved to be the most valuable hydraulic mines in the world, as the subsequent operations at North Bloomfield, Malakoff, Columbia Hill, Badger Hill, etc., demonstrated. Jackson and his Pard might have been tempted to a longer stay in the foothills had they had a glimmering of the possibilities.)

breaking up. The richest of it they spread out on the bare bed-rock and let it weather slack, and then pound it up with sledge hammers. In spite of all this they are making money. Over on the other side of the river, at Humbug, they have struck some good diggings and quite a large mining camp has sprung up there. It is a loose quartz gravel, easily washed, and they say that there are immense beds of it covering three or four miles up and down the ridge. It doesn't all pay; in fact, there are only a few spots that are rich enough to work, but there is a little gold through it all. If there was only some way to wash big quantities of it cheaply, there is lots of gold to be taken out.

Marie and I have paid a visit to Selby Flat, but I think we will avoid that place in the future. The boys treated us nicely and as respectful as could be; but the women—they are a lot of cats. There is not one of them that can hold a candle to Marie for good looks; and as for reputation, well, the most of them are good women, but there were a few who sneered behind our backs and were inclined to be very uppish, and those were the ones who had no reputation to speak of. All because she had dealt a gambling game and that is all they can say against her. I was inclined to give them a piece of my mind, but Marie laughed at it and said: "You foolish boy, never quarrel wiz a woman. You cannot fight wiz her and her tongue is too much for you." Of course, she is right; but it is this sort of thing that makes me want to get away from here. We have jolly times at the cabin, however. She always brings over some dainty to eat from the hotel or stores, and we get up all sorts of fancy dishes, that is, she does, and Pard and I do the rough work. She says cooking is an art in her country, and I guess it is, for she has about spoiled us and it would be a tough proposition to have to go back to our old grub. We have got down to coffee and bread for breakfast and neither one of us can tackle fried pork and beans any

more. It doesn't make much difference, as we do not get up until nine o'clock. Pard rolls out at daylight to fire rocks at the jackass, who insists on giving us an early concert every morning. We let Jack out to keep him company, and that seems to soothe his troubled spirit. It is a strange thing the attachment between the two animals. It's worth while being awakened to know that we have not got to crawl out, get breakfast and then tackle a hard day's work in the mud and water. Marie gets back to the hotel regularly before dark and won't let me stay later than ten o'clock. "It is for what ze people would say, my Alfred," and I strike out for the cabin. Pard is deep in his books, but he drops them and we chat and plan until midnight. We both wish the days would go by faster. The "old boy" is longing to see his wife and looking eagerly forward to the meeting.

Dunn and his partners put in the week on our Rock Creek claims and are well satisfied with the returns. They took in MacCalkins and Barker on the lay and six of them tackled it. It doesn't make any difference to us how many are interested, as we get twenty per cent. of what comes out. They cleaned up yesterday afternoon and had fifty-one ounces. That will give us two hundred dollars for our rake off and they are averaging about an ounce apiece per day. Dunn has an idea that he can do still better by increasing the size of the boxes. They are now using ten by twelve-inch bottoms and ten-inch sides. He has ordered at the mill two and a half feet bottoms and eighteen-inch sides of two inches thickness, and will set these in the bed of the creek, anchoring them down permanently so that flood water will not carry them away. He says he is convinced that if he can hold them down he can catch most of the gold in the dirt that is carried down when the water is high and then clean up the creek at low water. I do not see any reason why it should not work. Anyway, the experiment will cost us nothing.

Chinamen are getting to be altogether too plentiful in the country. Six months ago it was seldom one was seen, but lately gangs of them have been coming in from below. There is a big camp of them down on Deer Creek, below New-town, and we found a lot of them getting ready to work on the bars on the Yuba River. Pard and I chased a dozen off of our river claims and warned them that we would shoot them if we found them there again. We called a miners' meeting and adopted a miners' law that they should not be allowed to take up or hold ground for themselves nor should they mine worked or unworked ground unless purchased from a white owner. Some were for driving them out of the country entirely, but the majority thought it would be a good thing to sell them claims, as it was an easy way to make money. Pard says it is a great mistake to let them get any sort of a foothold; but as we are going to quit mining, our objections were not as strong as they might have been. I understand that most of the camps have adopted the same sort of law. They are not looked upon as human beings and have no rights that a white man is bound to respect, except in protecting them in their titles to ground that they have regularly bought under agreed conditions. Their big camp on Deer Creek was raided a couple of weeks ago, it is said, by a gang of Mexicans, two of them were killed and the remainder scattered all over the country. Report says that the Greasers got away with over thirty thousand dollars. The Chinamen appealed for protection, but nobody paid any attention to them. There were over fifty living in the camp and they ought to have been able to protect themselves; but they seem to be great cowards and will not fight under any circumstances.

I told Marie about my visit to the couple on Round Mountain and she proposed that we ride over and see them. We found them at home and still working the tunnel, and the man, while not particularly glad to see us, was decent enough

to ask us to get off of our horses and come inside the cabin. I don't think he liked the idea of Marie getting acquainted with the woman, although he made no objection. She was as shy as a deer and no doubt ashamed of her man's dress—she was still wearing overalls and shirt—and we left them together while he and I went outside for a chat. He was as curious as ever about what was going on outside and kept me busy for an hour posting him up to date on the news. Then we were called in to luncheon, which Marie had helped to get ready, and we had a nice meal. I noticed the woman's eyes were red and that she had been crying. Marie stepped on my foot and I had sense enough to say nothing awkward. When we bid them good-bye the women kissed each other and Marie promised to see her again soon. As soon as we were out of earshot she said indignantly: "Oh! he is what you call ze great brute; no, he does not beat her, she say he is not cruel, but she is all ze same as one prisoner and her heart it is for to break, she is so *isolement*—lonely you call it." They had had a long talk and, while the woman had not told her any of her history, or why she was leading so strange a life, she had learned enough to know that her solitude and isolation were not of her own choice. She said her work was really only play, that her companion did not ask her to toil, that her masculine dress was donned for convenience, and that they were making money and would go away when the claim was worked out. "There is ze grand mistarie," said Marie. "Oh, no, she is not ze wife of ze man and they hide away from ze world; more I do not know; she is for to keep her mouth shut, as you say in Engleesh. Some time there will be ze explosion, pouf! and then we will see." It is a queer case, but there is no call for outside interference that I can judge. I think that Marie is mistaken about her being a prisoner, as she has plenty of chances to go away if she wants to. I warned Marie not to talk about it, as it might make a lot of trouble for the couple when there was no call for it.

CHAPTER XXIV.

THE PARTNERS SELL OUT THE CREEK CLAIM—JACKSON'S REPUTATION IN HIS OLD HOME—PROVIDING FOR THE JACKASS'S FUTURE—THE SLOCUM FARM HAS NO ATTRACTION—LOAFING THE DAYS AWAY—RUSHES TO NEW LOCALITIES—TROUBLE ON ROUND MOUNTAIN—SCANDALMONGERS' TONGUES LET LOOSE—CHINAMEN SHOW FIGHT AND ARE RUN OFF OF DEER CREEK.

A FORTY-NINER

CHAPTER XXIV.

MAY 11, 1852.—The creek claim panned out well for the week, the clean-up yesterday amounting to sixty-one ounces. Dunn and his partners have been at the cabin all the afternoon bargaining to buy the claims outright, and we agreed on terms. They are to give us three thousand dollars in cash and we turn the ground over to them. This suits both of us, as we will go away next month and do not want any interests left behind, as neither of us calculate on coming back. As we have already agreed to sell our interests in the river claims for six thousand and are to receive our money on June 1, we will have nine thousand dollars to divide between us, which is not very bad for a winter's work.

I had some nice letters from home and a copy of the Winsted Herald, in which there is an item that Mr. Alfred Jackson, of Norfolk, had made his fortune in the California mines and would soon return and settle down in his old home. I guess the editor is mistaken about my settling down. Norfolk is too small a village for me, although there was a time when I thought it was the greatest place on earth. I am beginning to believe with Pard that this is going to be a great State, and the chances are that here will be my home. First, however, I am going to see something of the world; we will go to Europe and roam around for six months or more. Pard says it will be an ideal honeymoon trip and one that will expand my ideas, broaden me out, and that I will get rid of some of my Puritan notions. It may be so, but I guess my bring-

ing up has not been any great drawback. Come to think of it,
he has got as many queer ideas as I have. He has asked me
to give him Jack, which I am very glad to do. I like the old
dog mighty well, but somehow he was fonder of Pard from
the beginning, and besides, I could not very well take him to
the States with me. Then he is going to take the jackass
below with him; says he will turn him out on a ranch where
he can get a good living without work. He explained that he
could not bear to think of somebody packing him with heavy
loads over the rough trails and beating him to death. So he
is with all of God's creatures, a tender heart for everything
that lives.

For the past month everything has seemed as unreal to
me as a dream, and the thought comes once in a while that I
may wake up and find such to be the case. It is not quite three
years since I left home and the people wondered at my courage in venturing into an unknown country at the ends of the
earth. Now it seems as if it was the center of the universe
instead of the hub, and I have a sort of pity for those who are
ignorant of its attractions. I have become a reader and a
student. Books, which at one time were a weariness, delight
me. I came away engaged to be married to a good girl.
Now, although she is the same Hetty, I am not the same man,
and I know that we are not suited to each other. I was poor,
now I am comparatively rich, and I have ambitions and aspi-
rations to push on in the world and carve out a career, where
three years ago I would have been content to take the Slocum
farm and vegetate on it the rest of my life. I have faith that
Marie will not only make me a good wife, but also the companion I need as a stimulous to my ambitions. And then
Pard, who has been such a comfort and aid to me, made me
solemnly promise that when I get through with my wander-
ings I will come back to San Francisco and settle down there
where we can still have each other's friendship. He quotes

A FORTY-NINER

Emerson, "When you are sure of your friend, hold to him with hooks of steel." Well, it is a great change in three years and who knows what the next three years will bring?

MAY 18, 1852.—The days go by most pleasantly and we are almost as irresponsible as three children. The rains are over, the summer's heat has come and the foothills are an earthly paradise. We have even become too lazy to ride around the country. I content myself with an evening gallop to town and back, and the rest of the time we loaf under the trees. Pard quotes some old Greek poet about the Elysian Isles, "Where Rhadaman thus dwells, and pain and sorrow come not, nor rain or wind, and the never dying zephyrs blow softly off the ocean."

That will do very well just now, but it would not be very apt during one of our winter storms with a gale blowing through the pines, the limbs breaking and crashing to the ground, and everything in an uproar. I have a copy of Byron and am reading aloud his "Childe Harold." It is a great poem.

Nevada City is growing out of all bounds and is a big town. There are at least five thousand people living in and around it, and it is fast filling up with families from the States; wives and children come out to join their husbands. As a consequence, it is getting to be a much more orderly and decent community.

They nearly had a famine during the winter rains, but the roads are all in good order again and prices of all kinds of supplies reasonable. They are talking of building a wagon road over Sugar Loaf, down Rock Creek to the river, bridge that stream, and then over the Yuba divide to Cherokee and San Juan, both of which having grown to be good-sized and prosperous mining camps. The upper end of Shady Creek has paid well and good diggings have been found on Badger

Hill, but the best pay in that section has been taken out of Blind Shady, a gulch that empties into Big Shady Creek. I am told that there are a dozen claims on this ravine that have averaged a hundred dollars a day to the man. It does seem as if there was no end to the gold deposits. There has been a big rush to Gold Bluff, on the ocean beach above Trinidad, but most of the miners have come back badly disappointed. There were marvelous stories of the waves washing up dust on the beach by the bushel, but it was all an exaggeration. While there was some gold found, it was difficult to gather and in no such quantities as reported. It is curious how restless the majority of the miners are and how ready to pack up and drift away on the strength of mere rumors.

Marie is a prophet. There has been an explosion on Round Mountain and we can hardly get head or tail of it. Anyway, there was a shooting match, and nobody hurt, the woman has skipped the country with some other man and the one we thought her husband is back in the cabin alone, refusing to talk to anybody and more unsociable than ever. Marie saw the woman in Nevada with a stranger. They stayed there for a couple of days and then took the stage for parts unknown. From the little that the woman confided to Marie, the stranger called her companion out of the cabin and, after a few high words, drew a pistol and began shooting. He took to the brush and she did not think he was hit. Then she changed her dress, put on the clothes that belonged to her sex and came away with the new comer. She seemed to concede the stranger's right of possession, and was not unhappy. The sheriff went out to the cabin, the intruder having told him of the occurrence; expecting, possibly, to find a mortally wounded or dead man. On the contrary, he found the man unhurt and unwilling to give any details or make any complaint. There is a lot of gossip and talk over it and every man has a theory. The prevailing opinion is that the fellow had run away

with some man's wife, or mistress, and sought seclusion and concealment in their odd cabin on the mountain; that the wronged man had traced the guilty pair, tried to kill his wife's paramour, and, not succeeding, had to forgive her, taken her back and had gone away without any further attempt to avenge his wrongs, that is, if he had any to avenge. It's funny to hear the "cats" over at Selby Flat talk about it. Not one of them has a good word for the woman and think the husband must have been a mean spirited fellow in consenting to take her back. But, then, women have queer ways and don't see things in the same light that men do. They do say that the one who talks the most and the worst is badly tarred with the same stick. She has poked her nose into my affairs and I should have called her husband down long ago had it not been that we are going away soon and Pard's pleadings not to make a nasty rumpus over it.

The miners on Deer Creek, below the town, turned out last week and drove all of the Chinamen off that stream. The heathen had got to be impudent and aggressive, taking up claims the same as white men and appropriating water without asking leave. They cut one of the miner's dams and, when he attempted to repair it, chased him away, brandishing their shovels and making a great hullabaloo. He passed the word up and down the creek, and that afternoon about fifty miners gathered togther, ran the Chinamen out of the district, broke up their pumps and boxes, tore out their dams, destroyed their ditches, burned up their cabins and warned them not to come back under penalty of being shot if they made a reappearance. The miners' actions are generally endorsed and there is a disposition to bar the Chinks out of the district. It is said that they are coming to the State by thousands, and, if not molested, they would soon overrun the country. Below Newtown they have got possession of two or three miles of the creek and are not disturbed, as they ac-

quired the ground by purchase from white speculators. I am told that they paid in the neighborhood of forty thousand dollars for the claims they are working. It is a sight to see them on the trails, packing two big baskets of stuff on the ends of a bamboo pole and carrying a load that would stagger a jackass.

CHAPTER XXV.

SAD TERMINATION OF THE ROUND MOUNTAIN MYSTERY—A SUICIDE'S CYNICAL FAREWELL —THE INTRUSION OF THE "ETERNAL FEMININE"—PARD'S REMARKS—"LET THERE BE NO CLACK OF IDLE TONGUES"—AN IMPRESSIVE CEREMONY AND A SOLITARY GRAVE— THE PARTNERS GROW SENTIMENTAL OVER THE OLD LOG CABIN AND THEIR MUTUAL EXPERIENCES—PREPARING FOR A LEAVE-TAKING.

A FORTY-NINER

CHAPTER XXV.

MAY 25, 1852.—It would seem as if we had at last got to the final chapter in the story of the Round Mountain couple and it has ended in a sad sort of way. John Hall, who was out hunting yesterday afternoon, passed by the cabin and, seeing no signs of life and receiving no response to his call opened the door, which was unlocked, and went in. He was shocked to find the man on the bed lifeless and cold. There were no traces of violence and Hall says the man looked more like one asleep than dead. The cabin was undisturbed and if it had not been for a letter left on the table there would have been no reason to believe that he had died from other than natural causes. However, the note and the traces of crystals of arsenic in a cup clearly indicated that he had committed suicide. The letter, which I copied, was strange and pitiful. He had written in a clear, firm hand:

> *"Whoever finds my body, if it has not gone back to its original ele-*
> *"ments before discovery, will if it taxes not his humanity too much, dig a*
> *"hole and cover it with clean earth and there let it rot without mound or*
> *"stone to mark the place. It is only an atom that of its own accord goes*
> *"back from whence it came. While it dwelt on earth, it found men rogues*
> *"and women false. It inspired hate and treachery, but could not compass*
> *"love. Fearing its own company, distrusting all men and despising all*
> *"women, it arrogated the right to end an existence that was thrust upon*
> *"it without its consent. There is no one left to mourn or rejoice; and if*
> *"there is an unproved hereafter, of which no man knows, it will at least*
> *"have repose from the clack of idle tongues."*

There was no signature and, singularly enough, there was not a soul who knew the man's name. Pard, to whom I

read the copy of the letter, was quite affected and said that, while it was morbid and cynical, it showed, whoever he was, a man of more than ordinary intelligence, one who had drank the cup to the bitter dregs. "Be sure, Alf," he continued, "it's the eternal feminine; to some of us they are angels, to others —this poor fellow, for example—the reverse. I hope they will carry out his last wish, and I will go over this afternoon and see that they do." I went along and found quite a crowd. There was a coroner's inquest and a verdict of suicide, and then Pard proposed that we carry out the dead man's last request. We dug a hole on the hillside, about a hundred yards away from the cabin, rolled the body up in blankets and deposited it in the bottom. The crowd asked Pard to say something and he made a few remarks, in substance as follows:

"Boys, a sermon would be a hollow mockery, a eulogy pure invention, for of his virtues or his failings we know nothing. He was a man, who having tasted life, found it unpalatable and pushed it aside. From what little we know, he loved, sorrowed, despaired and laid down the burden. The only tribute we can pay him is to not vex the air roundabout his old dwelling place, to quote his epitaph, 'with the clack of idle tongues.'"

Then we filled the grave, rolled a big rock on it and went away. It was a simple but most impressive ceremony and one could see that it had made an impression on the crowd. Happy, careless fellows, they went from curiosity, and came away filled with great pity for the dead. After we got back to the cabin we could not help speculating on it all. Marie, who had stayed away, was in tears over the story and the last letter. "Poor fellow," she said, "perhaps somewhere a muzzer she wait and she mourn for him and he comes not." I rode over to town with her, but we were both low spirited and melancholy and had but little to say to each other. Altogether, it is about the saddest Sabbath day I have spent in this coun-

try, and it has set me thinking how little we know or care about the affairs of those other than ourselves or immediate friends.

JUNE 5, 1852.—In two weeks more we will bid the place goodbye and leave it, so far as I can see, for all time. I think we would go sooner, as we are all getting impatient and restless, but we will not receive the money for our river claims until the 8th of June and must wait to close that transaction. Dunn and company, who have bought and paid for our creek ground, are doing well, and are satisfied with the bargain. They have got the lumber on the ground for their big flume, half of the boxes made and will begin to put it in this week. They have also succeeded in buying up the most of Brush Creek below the flat and will flume it in the same way. All of the Saleratus Ranch boys are interested and I hope they will make a fortune. They are a jolly lot of fellows and, excepting Pard, my best friends, and they don't like to hear of our going away. Pard has planned to give a farewell supper to them and about twenty others, including Platt, Dixon, Gleason, and Fisk, our Rock Creek neighbors, and there he is going to carry out his intentions of telling them his right name and his reason for sailing under false colors, as he calls it. It will be a strictly stag affair, but even then Pard says men will tell their wives, wives will tell their neighbors, and there will be the "clack of idle tongues." We are going to give our books to the ranch boys, the rest of our belongings to our neighbors, and leave the old cabin to rot, or to the chance shelter of some wandering miner. As Pard says, it is humble enough and rude enough, but there is many a costly house that cannot compare with it, for it has sheltered and fostered enduring friendship, unruffled peace, the miracle of content and the boon of prosperity; and I add, a happy reconciliation, a growing romance, the awakening of love, and

we are a pair of soft chaps who grow sentimental over some rough pine logs and weather beaten shakes. I am sure, wherever we go, the old log cabin on Rock Creek will never fade out of our memory.

CHAPTER XXVI.

DISTRIBUTING PERSONAL EFFECTS—PARD'S FAREWELL DINNER—"ZEY ARE ZE GOOD BOYS."—CHAMPAGNE AND ITS EFFECTS—THE LAST SITTING UNDER THE OLD PINE TREE— VOICES OF THE NIGHT CHORUS A MELAN- CHOLY FAREWELL—WIND–UP OF JACKSON'S DIARY—THE FATE OF HETTY AND A LAST WORD IN REGARD TO THE ACTORS WHO HAVE FIGURED IN THE OLD-TIME RECORD.

A FORTY-NINER

CHAPTER XXVI.

JUNE 12, 1852.—Only a week more and it is good-bye to Rock Creek. We have arranged all our plans and will leave here on the 17th for San Francisco. Marie will take the stage and wait for us until we arrive, and will carry Jack along with her. The old dog will make no objection, as he is as fond of her as of us. Pard has arranged with a teamster to drive the jackass to Sacramento and we will ride that far on our horses and then take the boat. We calculate to reach the city by the 21st at the latest, and may get there a day earlier. Pard expects to meet his wife about the 23rd. She left New York, or was to, on the 25th of May. The old boy is as restless as a caged animal and paces up and down in front of the cabin until he has worn a path for a hundred feet or more, as well as wearing out Jack's patience. The dog started in to follow him, and it was fun to watch him look at Pard when he made the turn at each end. Jack soon gave it up as a piece of foolishness, this walking all the time and getting nowhere. It was an idiosyncrasy that he pardoned, but refused to be a party to, preferring to curl up alongside of Marie and be petted.

We have not got very much baggage to bother us. I have packed up all of the old letters and home trinkets and will send them by express. What little stuff we leave behind in the way of crockery, cooking utensils, etc., the neighbors are welcome to. I will give Calkins my shotgun and Charlie Barker my banjo. I have a pride in keeping up this diary to the last, and will write in it again next Sunday and carry it

221

with me in my saddle bags. We are going to have a blow-out at the Hotel de Paris Wednesday night, a sort of a farewell to those of our friends that we care to say good-bye to. Marie and the landlady are arranging for it, and we will surely have a good feast.

JUNE 17, 1852.—There are only six more blank pages in this book and I don't think I will fill them, neither will I start another one. I don't think I have written anything here that I would be ashamed to have my wife read. Pard has gone over it from start to finish and says that I ought to keep it until I am old and gray-haired. Then it will take on a new meaning and I will regret those glorious days when "youth was mine." I don't exactly catch his meaning, but it is certain that I shall look back to the old creek and the memories of it and its surroundings, and it will be a pleasant remembrance.

We had our dinner Wednesday evening and there were twenty-seven of us altogether, including the Saleratus Ranch boys and our neighbors. Marie looked in and helped the landlady awhile. There was real champagne, a couple of baskets of it, and before I knew it Pard had me by one arm and Marie by the other and the guests stood up and drank a toast to France and America and the pair whose prospective alliance would surely bring happiness to a representative of each country. I was too embarrassed to speak and the champagne choked me—it was the first time I had tasted it—but Marie bubbled over with glee and said, "Oh! zey are ze good boys, and in our hearts we will nevair, no nevair, forget zem," and then she ran away and was seen no more that night.

After she had gone Pard got up and made what he called his confession. He explained why he had taken the name of Anderson and, while he regretted the deceit, still there was no man in the world that he was ashamed to look in the face and he could only beg their pardon and return them a watch that

did not bear his name. You should have heard the shouting, everybody yelling: "No! No! Keep it and we will give you another one," crowding around and grasping his hand, and then MacCalkins yelled out: "What's in a name, anyhow?" Barker struck up:

> "For he's a jolly good fellow."

And we made the old hotel ring. Then we marched around the table, singing:

> "For he was a dandy man,
> With his rocker, pick and pan,
> And it took him quite a while
> Before he made his pile."

I don't remember much more about it. The table began to swim around, my head got dizzy. Pard took me out in the air, helped me on my horse, and we started home. My! I was sick on the way and the next morning my head ached to split. If that is the way champagne makes one feel, I don't want any more of it.

Pard and I sat out under the old pine tree to-night for the last time—we will be busy to-morrow getting our traps into town—and neither one of us was in the best of spirits, although as far as we can see there is nothing but happiness ahead of us. The moon beams shimmered down through the pine needles, the frogs croaked in the creek, a coyote barked up on the hill, the echo of the hoot of an owl drifted up from the trail. We have listened to the same sounds every night for years, but somehow this evening it seemed as if they were all saying "Good-bye."

THE DIARY OF

HERE THE DIARY ENDS.

(So we bid good-bye to Pard and Jackson, Marie and Hetty, Jack, the dog, and the donkey, to "ze good boys" of Rock and Brush Creeks. The days of placer mining, as depicted in the diary, came to an end long ago, the glory of Selby Flat, that once "beat Nevada City in a Fourth of July celebration" has departed; even the patient Chinamen glean no more from the worked-out creeks, gulches and ravines. The romance and the sordid facts are but dim memories and the Argonauts have gone to seek the golden fleece in the land just beyond the sunset.

They were good old days and when Jackson forgot to put his diary in the saddle bags he left for posterity a record unique and invaluable. We have had a surfeit of the stoic gambler, uncouth miner, draggled-tailed courtesans and impossible school mistresses. These were inventions touched, distorted and illuminated by Bret Harte's genius. The later day writers who attempt to reproduce this early life with their sentimental pathos are as far away from the spirit of the "Fifties" as mush and molasses from "Lobster a la Newburg." While Jackson's narrative may not rank high as literature, he has given in his diary a faithful, accurate, and vivid picture, from the miner's point of view, of foothill mining life. As he was writing it for his own amusement and not for posterity, the weaving into it of his romance is to be pardoned. For myself, I confess that to me this has been one of its chief fascinations. Its great interest, however, is the details we glean of the everyday life, of how much yellow dust the claim yielded, the growth of mining camps, the queer theories as to the genesis of gold, the incidents and happenings in town and country, the comedies and tragedies; these constitute history not to be found elsewhere. Yet, to note the gradual development and mental growth of this New England Puri-

tan, the intrusion of "the eternal feminine," the hesitation and doubt, the surrender and final culmination of it at the point most novelists end the final chapter, the marriage altar, surely that was a romance of the foothills. However, all this had best be left to the reader. I trust that he has been as much entertained in following Jackson's fortunes as I in deciphering and transcribing them from the blotted pages and faded ink of his old diary.

A final word. Nevada pioneers will recall many of the men who figure in the diary. John Hall, John Dunn, Henry Shively, Barker, the Calkins, these were all Forty-niners, well known in local annals. Niles Searls, Tom Williams, Frank Dunn, Stanton Buckner—whose dignity was so badly ruffled by "Rattlesnake Dick"—were members of the bar, and Zeno P. Davis, the gunsmith, was a familiar character. The brick courthouse, that was pronounced an extravagance because there would be no use for it after the gold gave out, is replaced by a still more costly one. The "Hotel de Paris" flourished until late in the sixties, and the quartz veins, so quaintly described as white rock with gold in it, are still yielding treasure. Rock and Brush Creeks are overgrown and choked with growth of alder and willow, the pines that towered above the rude log cabin were felled long ago and a second growth takes their place, the old trails replaced by dusty highways; yet the coyotes bark, the frogs croak, and the owls hoot in chorus, as when Jack interpreted it all as a "good-bye." The flourishing mining camps that he visited, the euphonious "Red Dog," Cherokee, Humbug, Rough and Ready, You Bet, Coyoteville, and Blue Tent, are but travesties of the old times; even "Lousy Level" is known no more. I am sure we are indebted to Jackson in so far as his diary gives us a glimpse of those golden days.

Moved by a spirit of curiosity as to the later career of Jackson, I made inquiries by letter at his old home, Norfolk,

Connecticut. I did not get much information from my corre-spondent—woman, by the way—but enough to determine that Jackson did not return to tarry in that placid village. She said that a family of Jacksons lived on Pond Hill, about a mile from the town, on a farm; that they had sold the property just before the war, left the State, and it was said that San Francisco was their destination. They had a son who had made a fortune in California and had come back on a visit, accompanied by his wife, a foreign woman (mark the contempt of the phrase), and that was all she knew of the Jacksons. She devoted a dozen pages to that interesting girl, Hetty North, which I will try to condense into as many lines. The Norths were prominent people of Colebrook township. Hetty was accomplished, her education was finished off in the Hartford Seminary, she played the melodeon, was a handsome, black-haired, black-eyed beauty, and had taught school at Cole-brook Center. In 1860 she married a prosperous farmer and then went, not exactly crazy, but eccentric; embraced spiritu-alism and all the other "isms" of the time. Some four years before her death, she took to her bed, although affected with no malady, and there she resolutely remained until her dying day. In the light of this I think Jackson is to be congratulated on his escape, and I doubt not that he was far happier with the "foreign woman." As for Anderson, it has been explained in a previous note that he became a leader in the State as a lawyer, politician, orator, and millionaire, and that for reasons heretofore given it is better that his identity should remain undisclosed.)

THE END.

A FORTY-NINER

EPILOGUE.

The publication of "THE DIARY OF A 49r" was interrupted and delayed by a catastrophe that for a brief time put aside all interest in literary matters. On the morning of April 18 occurred the violent earthquake and the beginning of the fire, that within three days reduced San Francisco to ashes. When the conflagration ceased, the city had reverted almost to its original conditions, when, as the pueblo of Yerba Buena, it was a cluster of adobe houses and had not reached sufficient importance to be dignified by location on a map. The compiler of "The Diary" had watched it from its earliest beginnings, through all its growth and transformation into an important city. As the outlines of the hills and valleys that formed its sight came into view and its desolation was realized it came to the few left of us, old pioneers, how much we loved the place and with what sentiment we regarded it. We did not mourn the destruction of the modern fourteen-story buildings, the big business blocks of later years, or the fine residences of the Western Addition; but there were old shacks, dilapidated houses, one-story shanties that had not given away to modern progress, and that told of the life and the old days. When they were built we were young men, who in all of the ups and downs of the town, the fires that devastated it, the exodus to other fields where new gold discoveries had been made and which threatened to depopulate the city, the wane of gold products, wet seasons and dry seasons, had kept our faith in its ultimate grand destiny, and we saw our courage justified and our predictions close to fulfillment,

when, a little rocking of the earth, and behold! it was blotted out.

In that fateful forty-eight seconds, the numbed and paralyzed by the crash and wreck, the dull, sinister roar that seemed to be nature's threat to end all things, the menace that some malign power added as a dirge to the death throes of the world, there flitted through our brain the questioning thought as to whether it was a continental cataclysm, or a mere local disturbance. Were the old Sierras shaken to their foundation and undergoing a remoulding such as characterized the era when her mighty rivers were buried a thousand feet deep in lava? Was it another upheaval of the more recent coast range, or a new mountain-making process? There was a tinge of regret, even in that moment of supreme peril, that the works of the upbuilder should come to naught. It was local and the foothills are still there. At least, us old boys, who counted in our memories as the red-letter day in our lives those we spent in the "Fifties" on the western slopes of the Sierra Nevada range, had a harbor of refuge and it would not be much of a hardship if we driven back to our early haunts. To be sure, the ounce diggings were gone, the cabins had rotted away, the unsightly scars we had left when we had overturned the flats, bars and hillsides in our search for gold had taken on a new aspect, for nature, ever laboring to restore the original condition, had renewed the soil and replanted the barren wastes. The balmy air, the swaying pines, the spreading oaks invited us to peace and the simple life. Would it not be better to gather together what remained to us, get back to the foothills and pass the remainder of our days in idle contentment? Of course, it was only a dream, although an alluring one, and none will desert the city in its extremity.

Sturdy Jackson and his old "Pard" are resting in Lone Mountain Cemetery and the overturning and shattering of their monuments did not disturb their slumber. The city they

A FORTY-NINER

helped to build is ashes and debris, but their pioneer spirit still lives and animates their descendants, and doubtless the same steadfast purpose that created a prosperous commonwealth will be equal to the reconstruction of the destroyed city. It will not be the "Bay," as we miners used to term it—that will live only in our memories for the brief time that we linger and in the legends and traditions passed on to our descendants. The hurly-burly of the "Fifties," that strange mixture of discordant elements, that life that had almost resolved itself into its primitive beginnings, that levelling of social standards that put us all on an equality, the freedom from the thousand vexatious trammels of our modern business methods, the days of the circulation of the slug (a locally-coined gold piece valued at fifty dollars) and when our smallest coin was a two-bit piece, when strength and muscle counted for more than brains, when the scarcity of good women elevated them in our esteem to goddesses, and to whom we paid a profound and sincere deference very much modified in these modern times—all of these characteristics vanished in the long ago and with the atmosphere that made San Francisco unique.

Since the earthquake it has been current comment that the city had reverted to "Forty-nine" conditions; but we old fellows know better than that. There is not the least resemblance, except in one or two disastrous fires in '50 and '51 when we took on sackcloth and ashes for a brief time. The ruins are picturesque in their desolation, but they are a mass of twisted iron beams, fallen brick and stone, tangled electric and telephone wires—all betraying modernity. When we were burned out in the "Fifties" there were no debris problems confronting us, there was nothing but ashes and the gentle trade winds that swept them into the bay. Those who allude to the resemblance to a '49 camp are of the ilk that we term "Pullman Car Pioneers," who make their sightseeing pilgrim-

age on the restored trolley car lines, or dash over the paved streets in automobiles where we plodded in mud ankle-deep or rode a bucking mustang across the drifting sandhills.

Glory be! the foothills are as firm on their granite base as in the days when served by youth we built our cabins beneath lofty sugar pines, baked our bread in the Dutch ovens, ate our primitively cooked meals on rough planked tables, smoked our pipes in the gathering twilight while we discussed with our neighbors the luck of the day, or took the trails for the nearest camp in search of relaxation and distraction from the monotony of our toil. We fancied then that we were martyrs; that we were enduring hardships, exposure and wearisome banishment; that there were no compensations except "striking it rich," not realizing that we were having the "time of our lives," and that, in future years, we would, like Jackson, evoke from out of the past pleasant recollections of the log-cabin, the claim in the gulch and ravine, the care-free hours, when we accounted to no one either in the matter of our habits or our pleasures, when hospitality and good-fellowship were the rule, when nobody fawned on the rich or flouted the poor—yes, they were golden, unmatchable days, and when we old boys get together we are prone to grow garrulous and rather pity these young fellows, our descendants, who know nothing of that era of steamer days, of Broadway Wharf and the tide of sturdy humanity that gathered there every afternoon on its way to the mines, crowding the Sacramento and Stockton boats; of that favorite hostelry, the What Cheer house, where the majority of the visiting miners put up and which would not accept women as guests; of the hundred landmarks that have been swept away. With them has gone all that made San Francisco dear to us; and, while we admire their courage, energy, fortitude and optimism—concede that they inherit the spirit that possessed and was typical of the "Argonaut"—we shake our

A FORTY-NINER

heads and bid good-bye to the last link of the golden age. Our memories were of "when the water came up to Montgomery Street"; now our successors will date of the time "when the fire reached Van Ness Avenue."

C. L. CANFIELD.

San Francisco, Cal., August 1, 1906.